KT-553-929

SAGE
Study Skills

The Good Writing Guide for Education Students

Dominic Wyse

SAGE Publications

London • Thousand Oaks • New Delhi

© Dominic Wyse 2006

First published 2006

Apart from any fair dealing for the purposes of research or
private study, or criticism or review, as permitted under
the Copyright, Designs and Patents Act, 1988, this publication
may be reproduced, stored or transmitted in any form,
or by any means, only with the prior permission in writing
of the publishers, or in the case of reprographic reproduction,
in accordance with the terms of licences issued by the
Copyright Licensing Agency. Enquiries concerning reproduction
outside those terms should be sent to the publishers.

SAGE Publications Ltd.
1 Oliver's Yard
55 City Road
London EC1Y 1SP

SAGE Publications Inc
2455 Teller Road
Thousand Oaks, California 91320

SAGE Publications India Pvt Ltd
B-42, Panchsheel Enclave
Post Box 4109
New Delhi 110 017

British Library Cataloguing in Publication data

A catalogue record for this book is available
from the British Library

ISBN-10 1-4129-1983-5   ISBN-13 978-1-4129-1983-8
ISBN-10 1-4129-1984-3 (pbk)   ISBN-13 978-1-4129-1984-5 (pbk)

Library of Congress Control Number: 2005936263

Typeset by C&M Digitals (P) Ltd., Chennai, India
Printed in Great Britain by the Cromwell Press, Trowbridge, Wiltshire
Printed on paper from sustainable resources

511· 502821

The Good Writing Guide for Education Students

DISCARDED

Loughborough College

LC040989

Contents

Acknowledgements

My very grateful thanks to all the students whose work is featured in the book, they were an inspiration to me.

I would very much like to thank Jude Bowen for the work that we have done together in the past and once again for her expert editing during the publishing of this book. I also wish to pay tribute to Eve Bearne's influential contribution to the literacy field and for her inciteful foreword to this book. My warm appreciation also goes to Rebecca de Luca Wilson and Jeanette Graham for negotiating through the minefield of different styles, and to Charlotte Saunders.

This book is dedicated to Steven Ford for his contribution in the form of a 15 year argument about grammar and for the two puzzles in the grammar chapter. It is also dedicated with fondness to the memory of Charlie Ford who was never short of a viola joke.

Foreword

The Good Writing Guide for Education Students speaks directly to students of education. One of its strengths is that it acknowledges that writing about teaching, about educational theory, about policy, practice and classroom research all make different demands. Other books about studying at graduate and post-graduate level do not give the student teacher the specific guidance provided here. The examples are all drawn from genuine student work about familiar educational topics so that this book provides unique support for trainee teachers wishing to improve their knowledge and expertise.

Dominic Wyse writes in an accessible, direct style as he tackles the problems and possibilities of reading, researching and writing for education courses. He provides clear guidance about using the internet as well as books and journals and because of his experience as a teacher, researcher and writer he is able to direct students to the most useful sources. But this is not a book about short cuts. Wyse emphasises the importance of thorough and thoughtful reading and research as well as the value of students finding ways of reading their own work critically and attentively. His advice about developing an ear for writing is particularly valuable.

The Good Writing Guide for Education Students is more than a guide to effective study. Besides offering practical suggestions, there is a wealth of useful information about language which provides readers with the essential background to improving their own performance. Students at any stage of their education courses and at any level of confidence and assurance in their own writing will find it an invaluable resource.

Eve Bearne
Senior Associate, University of Cambridge Faculty of Education

How to use this book

This book will help you to improve your writing. It has been written particularly for people who are studying education: the topics and examples have been chosen with those students in mind. However, students from a wider range of subjects will also find much in the book that will help them.

The book is divided into two parts. Part I helps you to see that good writing is closely linked with reading and thinking. Reading and thinking precede good writing but they also continue during the writing process itself. The nuts and bolts of the writing process are the focus for Part II.

One way to use this book is to read it all, think about the ideas and then try some of them when you do your next piece of writing. Another way to use the book would be to check the summaries at the beginning of each chapter to find a topic that is of most interest to you, read the chapter, then try the ideas. The numerous examples of students' writing will enable you to compare your work with theirs. These will help you to realise that writing is hard work for all writers but it is something that becomes much easier with practice and thought.

The chapters begin with an overview of the topic. Key principles are outlined which should be used to guide your writing. To complement the text of the overviews, 'top tips' are offered to give you quick advice which, if you adopt them, will lead to quick improvements. The book also includes 'key facts' throughout. These will help to focus your mind on the essence of the concepts that are being covered. The final part of each chapter includes 'dos and don'ts' which help you to avoid common pitfalls.

What if you don't understand a particular term? The glossary at the end of the book consolidates and adds to the key facts to help you with this. The words included in the glossary are denoted with this symbol **G** on their first occurrence in the book. And don't forget the index – you might find that a quick search in the index could save you a lot of time when trying to find a particular piece of advice about writing.

Finally, bear in mind that writers and publishers have different ways of doing things. For instance, there is more than one way to reference and to use some punctuation marks. Whether or not you follow my advice on these aspects, it is important to apply your chosen style consistently.

By buying this book you have already done something positive; you've said to yourself 'I want to improve my writing'. If you take on board the messages from the book and apply them to your own writing you will see your writing going from strength to strength, and so will your tutors!

Part I   Reading and Thinking

1 Reading Widely

The single most important thing that you can do to improve the chances of success on your course is to read widely. In order to help you to do that this chapter gives guidance on the qualities of the different kinds of texts that you will read and explains why some are likely to help more than others. The important concept of *peer-review* Ⓖ is introduced in relation to internet texts, academic journals and books.

You may have heard stories about people with no previous experience suddenly writing a bestseller. One day they sit down and, without planning, write for about six weeks solid, until a book is complete. With very little effort they become rich beyond their wildest dreams. Do not believe these stories! When you look into the background of any successful writer there is a history of writing experience behind them. It may be that they kept a diary; or perhaps they wrote a travel journal for each holiday, or edited a school fanzine; it may be that they worked as a journalist, a teacher, an academic or some other job that required regular writing. Whatever their background, all professional writers succeed by very determined hard work, the ability to learn from their failures and the understanding that becoming a good writer takes time.

Thankfully you do not have to become a professional writer in order to succeed on your course, however there are lessons that can be learned from these people. What all writers have in common is that they have practised the craft of writing. But just as important, they have read widely the kinds of texts that they intend to write. This shows us that if you want to write brilliant assignments you need to read similar texts. Examples from previous years' students can be helpful but in particular you should read published books and papers by experts in your subject. This is the kind of writing that is the best model for your own.

As a student on a course you have to read for three reasons:

- Texts contain the knowledge that you need to understand as part of your course.

- Texts give clues to how you should write.

- Wide reading will result in higher marks for your assignments.

Points one and three are related. Any formal course assessment is designed to assess the level of your understanding of a particular topic. The knowledge required for the highest levels of understanding is contained in published texts. Therefore you have to read these texts and show that you have fully understood them to achieve the highest marks.

However, the point that I want to emphasise is point two: you must learn to read like a writer. After you have read a text to understand more about your subject, read it again in a different way. Read it with questions like these in mind:

- Who is the writer's main audience?

- What issues has the writer chosen to cover?

- If I list the main issues does it help me understand the piece better?

- How does the writer organise the text?

- How do they use subheadings?

- What particular words and phrases do they use?

- How do they refer to other people's work?

- What makes the first sentence/first paragraph effective?

- What kinds of texts are listed in the reference list; which ones shall I read next?

- How do they start the text?

- How do they end the text?

★ TOP TIP

Read texts yourself first hand (the *primary source* ⑥)not by reading another text (a *secondary source* ⑥) referring to the primary source.

The relevance of wide reading to academic assignments is perhaps more obvious than to assignments that focus on practical teaching and evaluation. You might question how wide reading improves these teaching evaluations. Your own views and reflections on your practical work are important, but you also need to challenge your opinions by comparing them with the opinions of others. Often, people who publish texts about education have taught for many years in a variety of settings so they are likely to have more experience to draw on than you. This means that they often understand the issues in greater depth. When you read and understand their work you can benefit from their knowledge and will subsequently understand the subject in greater depth yourself.

Where to start your reading

A tutor's *reading list* is a very good place to start. If the list is good it will be up-to-date and will recommend texts that are at the appropriate level for you. However, students frequently find that key books on the reading list have already been borrowed from the library. If you find yourself in this situation don't despair, there are various ways round it. Although your tutor will recommend specific texts, the authors of these are likely to have published other texts that might be useful. You can do a search under the author's name (see Chapter 2) to find other things that they have published. Perhaps even more important than this is to remember that journals cannot be taken out of the library so you will always be able to access them. More and more these are available electronically so you can sometimes access them from your home. Another option, apart from books and papers, is the internet. But before you decide which kind of text to read you need to understand about the qualities of different texts.

⚷ KEY FACT

A *paper* Ⓖ is an article published in an academic journal. Some papers are presented at academic conferences prior to publication.

The internet is a potentially useful source of information but it can also lead to misunderstanding and weak writing. The *Times Educational Supplement* (TES), which can be found online, is a good example. The TES is a weekly summary of current events in education. The online archives also allow you to search for previous news. Let's say that you have been asked to carry out an assignment with the topic of assessment. On 13 May 2005 Joseph Lee published an interesting article in the TES about the 'hysteria' caused by a government report which claimed that too many children were not learning to read. The TES article is helpful because it alerts you to the report from government. The article also makes the important point that children who achieve level 3 are not 'failing', they are actually pretty good readers. But, although this has some useful information it is not as rigorous as a good academic journal article.

★ **TOP TIP**

Make sure you know the right way to refer to media articles:

Inappropriate: 'Eboda (2004) shows that institutional racism is present in teams of football commentators'. While this may or may not be true the citation (see Chapter 3) is to a journalist who wrote a newspaper article not a researcher who has published evidence on the issue.

Appropriate: 'The issue of racism has been highlighted in the press recently in an *Observer* newspaper article' (Eboda, 2004). This comments on the way the newspaper covered the issue rather than using the newspaper as an authoritative source to support a point.

Journals

Let's look at our topic of assessment from the perspective of a good research journal. Peter Tymms asked the question 'Are standards rising in English primary schools?' and he published the answer to this question in an article in the highly regarded *British Educational Research Journal*. He concluded that independent measures showed that the gains shown in statutory test results (often called SATs) between 1995 and 2000 were not nearly as strong as some people were claiming and that after 2000 there was no further progress (Tymms, 2004). The important point that I want to make here is that in order to get his article published Peter Tymms had to wait until two or more experts in the field had read it and decided if it was good enough to be published. Ideally this process should be 'blind': in other words the referees do not know who has written the paper (some journals even require references to the authors' own work in the reference list to be disguised or removed). The whole process is called peer-review and it is the way that we ensure that knowledge that is published is accurate and significant. It doesn't just apply to education, it applies to all subjects that each have their own specialist journals. Therefore if you want to support your points with reference to a published text you are better choosing peer-reviewed articles in good journals.

Although the *British Educational Research Journal* is excellent, it is unlikely to be the place where you will start your reading because the articles are written at the level of professional researchers and academics. Peer-reviewed journals differ in the level of writing and the rigour of their peer-review procedures. For example the journal *Education 3–13* is also peer-reviewed but not in the same way that the *British Educational Research Journal* is. It also tends to cover more professional topics and is written in a way that you will probably find easier to read in the early stages of your course.

Books

The better journals explain the way that they peer-review articles as part of their 'information for contributors' which is how we know that they are peer-reviewed. For books things are a little more complicated. Most education publishers require authors to prepare a proposal for a book (and often a sample chapter) which is then sent to referees. The proposal is sent, not the complete text of the book. This means that what the author writes in the book if it is published is *not* peer-reviewed. Some publishers do send complete texts to be peer-reviewed and the author then has to respond to any suggested changes. But it is very difficult for you to know which publishers are the most rigorous. Publishers of books also use likely readers of the book as peer-reviewers who will have very helpful views about how to make it user-friendly but usually do not have the same academic expertise as other peer-reviewers.

Books can be very useful because they give the author space to cover a wider range of topics in great depth. This means that a really good recently published book can give you a very good overview of *the field* **©**. This can be a very useful starting point for your reading, although locating such a book is not always easy.

⚸ KEY FACT

'The field' means an area of study.

If you find this kind of book it should have an up-to-date reference list which means that you can choose some of the references to read first hand.

The word *handbook* **ᴳ** when used as part of the title for an academic book can be important. The word has a different meaning from the everyday idea of a handy book. A really good academic handbook is typically international in scope so will have contributors from around the world who are experts in the field. It also attempts to be comprehensive in order to establish a clear picture of the field at a particular moment in time. These books are usually edited collections which means that an editor or editors will have invited contributors to send in a chapter. The editors will then offer comments about the chapter to encourage the contributor to improve it and to ensure it fits well with the aims of the book. The editors and the contributors will already have a track-record in the field and will usually have published widely so you can have more confidence that this kind of book is academically rigorous.

★ TOP TIP

Work towards using journal articles more than books to support the points in your assignments.

If you find that when you read some articles and some books they seem to be very difficult to understand, don't worry. Part of the process of learning is the growing ability to cope with more and more demanding texts. When I started work on my Master's degree I was advised to read research methodology articles. At first it was as if some of the articles were written in a completely different language because I could barely understand them. In a way, you could say that they *are* written in a different language. The highest levels of writing in a subject use short key phrases to summarise complex ideas. The writers assume that their audience has a knowledge of the field so will not need certain things explaining. In other words, all subjects have *jargon* **ᴳ**. When you read the word 'jargon' you probably think about it negatively as something that people use just to sound good. It is true that jargon can be used sloppily. But when used well it saves writers having to explain particular concepts in full and at length.

The final distinction that I want you to understand is the difference between texts which give guidance about practice and those which are more theoretical and include research findings. The practical books will be useful if your assignment expects you to show that you can think clearly about your practice. The more theoretical books can be used as a *citation* ❻ (see Chapter 3) to support your academic arguments in an assignment. Some books are very good at mixing theory, research and practice although these are less common. Typically you will find that in education assignments you need to use a mixture of theoretical and practical sources.

DOS AND DON'TS

✓ Do

- read texts yourself first-hand rather than relying on secondary sources

- use the internet in the early stages of an assignment to help you get to grips with the main issues

- read recently published texts before you move to older texts

✗ Don't

- use newspaper articles to academically support the points that you are making in an assignment

- leave your reading until the last minute

- rely too heavily on one text

2 Searching for Reading Materials

The choice of the most appropriate texts is a very important part of writing a good assignment. In order to find these texts you need to have effective strategies for *searching* Ⓖ. This chapter explains how you can use library computer catalogues and the British Educational Index to make your searches more efficient.

In Chapter 1 I suggested that your tutor's recommendations are a good starting point for your reading when preparing for an assignment. However, you might well ask which text do I start with? My advice is to start with one of the most recently published ones. If the author has done their job properly the text will include a really good reference list with a range of work in the field which you can follow up.

★ TOP TIP

The first text(s) that you read should be from the same year in which you are doing your work. Look for the year of publication of the article or book. Try and find a text published in the same year in which you are working. If you can't then try the year before, and so on.

Let's now think about other ways to search for texts. The most basic search involves going to the library and looking along the shelves. Although I am going to show that there are better ways to search than this, there is one advantage of looking at the books on a library shelf. If you browse the titles and check the contents occasionally you do at least get a feel for the kinds of issues that are being covered by books in the field. The big limitation of this method is that there are likely to be many books which have been taken out of the library by other students.

Another basic search involves visiting your local bookshop to see which books are available on the shelves. Publishers' websites are an important part of this way of searching and sometimes offer free download materials. Internet bookshops such as Amazon allow you to search by simple categories of books which can also help in the early stages.

A more efficient search can be done by using the library computer catalogue. Library catalogues (like all search tools) work on *keyword* ☉ searches of titles, authors and other bibliographic information.

★ TOP TIP

If you cannot find the exact text on your tutor's reading list try a search for the author's name. This could help you find other texts that are relevant.

⚷ KEY FACT

A keyword or keywords will describe the topic that you are working on. *Search engines* identify keywords in computer files that hold information about texts.

Most library catalogues work in similar ways so I have chosen the one at the University of Cambridge as an example because it is the one that I currently use.

⚸ KEY FACT

Cambridge Library is called a Legal Deposit Library (previously called a copyright library). It keeps one copy of each edition of every book published in the United Kingdom and tries to conserve them forever. There are five Legal Deposit Libraries in the British Isles:

- Bodleian Library, Oxford
- Cambridge University Library
- National Library of Scotland
- Library of Trinity College Dublin
- National Library of Wales

The library catalogue at Cambridge has a basic search and a more advanced search which is called a *Guided Search*. There are many different libraries which are connected at Cambridge. The faculty of education library can be accessed as part of a search which is restricted to an A to E listing of Cambridge libraries. The search window shows a box for your keywords and some categories which you can choose:

Keyword Anywhere – will search for your keyword in any part of the library record for a text;

Author – will search for the name of an author;

Title – will search for the title of a text;

Journal Title – this helps you to search for journals that are in the library;

Subject Heading – libraries assign their own keywords reflecting the subject that texts cover;

Boolean Search – enables you to combine keywords using 'and', 'or' or 'not'; for example, 'grammar' and 'teaching';

Classmark – a code which indicates where you will find the text on the shelves;

Date – publication date.

Let's choose a subject that you might be preparing for an assignment: the teaching of grammar in primary classrooms. A basic search for title using the keyword 'grammar' reveals a range of texts (see Figure 2.1).

Next you have to think about which of the entries might be most useful so that you can avoid wasting time on irrelevant items. Table 2.1 explains how I would think about this in relation to the search shown in Figure 2.1.

Table 2.1   Relevance of items in initial search for term 'Grammar'

Item Number	Thoughts on relevance of text
Items 1, 2, and 3	Publication date too old as a starting point for reading.
4	Full library record reveals that this is mainly about secondary education.
5	Might have some useful information but library record not sufficient to make decision. Would be worth having a quick look and checking contents page.
6, 8, and 9	History focus; revealed by the information about library location, for example, 'Anglo-Saxon, Norse & Celtic Library'.
7	Gender as a topic may be too specific at this stage.
10	More about assessment than the teaching of grammar.

Figure 2.1   Cambridge University Library Catalogue Basic Search

So from the first 10 items in the list, number five is the only one that I might check. However, if we use a better search strategy we might get some more relevant references. Here's what happened when I used the combination of 'grammar' and 'teaching' in the more advanced 'guided search' which allows you to combine keywords in more than one search box (Figure 2.2).

The first two entries appear to be about practice so would be worth a look if this was the main focus of your assignment. But what about texts that report research? The *Grammar Papers* was published by the Qualifications and Curriculum Authority (QCA), so normally you expect this to be about government curriculum policy because that is the role of the QCA. However, the publication is a collection of papers which came out of a conference that the QCA organised. One of these papers is a review of research into the teaching and learning of grammar (although unusually the author is not named). This is a useful text that I would definitely want to read for the assignment because not only does it cover research but it is also related to policy.

Overall you can see that our brief search for books has given us two reasonable possibilities so far. In addition to reading them and recording some of the information (see later in this chapter) you should also check their reference lists, and follow up some of the useful ones to find further reading materials.

The main thing that the library catalogue search cannot locate is chapters about the teaching of grammar in edited books. For example you often find that academic handbooks on the subject of the teaching of English may include a chapter on grammar but library catalogues do not include the contents of books in their records. The only way that you can find these using a library catalogue is to make an assumption based on the title. For example if the book was called *Teaching English, Language and Literacy* you would expect there to be a chapter on grammar. The other way to find chapters in edited books is if they are included in the reference list of another text.

Multimap IF BEI Electronic Resources Google Scholar Trainline AltaVista Webmail Apple Mac Amazon eBay Yahoo! News ▾

http://depfacae-newton.lib.cam.ac.uk/cgi-bin/Pwebrecon.cgi?SA81=grammar&BOOL1=all+of+the Q▾ Google

Database Name: Department & Faculty Libraries A-E
Search Request: Advanced Search = (grammar)[in Title] AND ("teaching")[in Title]
Search Results: Displaying 1 through 8 of 8 entries.

[previous] [next]

Sort by: [⊡]   [Post Limit]

#	Title Long	Author	Date
□ [1]	Effective grammar teaching : an active approach / Heather Rendall.	Rendall, Heather.	2000
	Library Location: Education Faculty Library *Classmark: 407 REN*	*Status: Not On Loan*	
□ [2]	English grammar and teaching strategies : lifeline to literacy / Joy Pollock and Elisabeth Waller.	Pollock, Joy, 1927-	2000
	Library Location: Education Faculty Library *Classmark: 425 POL*	*Status: On Loan*	
□ [3]	Grammar papers : perspectives on the teaching of grammar in the National Curriculum / Qualifications and Curriculum Authority.	Qualifications and Curriculum Authority.	1998
	Library Location: EDU Cataloguing Desk *Classmark: 420.07 QUA*	*Status: Not On Loan*	
□ [4]	Higher teaching of Latin grammar in Ireland during the ninth century.	Draak, M.	1967
	Library Location: Anglo-Saxon, Norse & Celtic Library *Classmark: E 185 DRA*	*Status: Not On Loan*	
□ [5]	Not whether but how : teaching grammar in English at key stages 3 and 4 1999 / Qualifications and Curriculum Authority.		1999
	Library Location: Education Faculty Library *Classmark: 425 QUA*	*Status: Not On Loan*	
□ [6]	Teaching and learning grammar / Alison Taylor.	Taylor, Alison.	1994
	Library Location: Education Faculty Library: Temporary Reference Collection *Classmark: 40713 CON*	*Status: Not On Loan*	
□ [7]	Teaching grammar: a guide for the national curriculum.	Hudson, R.A.	1992
	Library Location: Education Faculty Library *Classmark: 425 HUD*	*Status: Not On Loan*	
□ [8]	Teaching grammar communicatively / Sue Purcell	Purcell, Sue.	1997
	Library Location: Education Faculty Library: Available on request *Classmark: 410/07 PUR*	*Status: Not On Loan*	

Figure 2.2   Cambridge University Library Catalogue Guided Search

> **⚘ KEY FACT**
>
> Although a book called a 'handbook' sounds like it should be a relatively easy read this is not usually the case. An academic handbook is intended to represent some of the best scholarship in the field.

Although library catalogue searches are a good strategy in the early stages of preparation for an assignment there are other more sophisticated ways that, once you are familiar with them, could save you time. It is also the case that as you progress towards the final stages of your course there is an expectation that your reading will be carried out in more depth which will require better search strategies.

The British Educational Index

One of the most useful tools for education students is the *British Educational Index* (BREI) ⊜ online hosted by *Dialog Datastar*. This enables you to find titles of nearly all peer-reviewed journal articles and theses (and some non peer-reviewed work) in education from 1976 onwards. Most university education libraries subscribe to this service. You can normally access it on-campus, or at home with what is called an 'Athens' password.

Indices like the BREI all work in a similar way by requiring keyword searches. You will probably be familiar with keyword searches on the internet using search engines ⊜ like *Google* or *AltaVista* and, if so, will be aware how difficult it can sometimes be to find the particular piece of information that you want. This can also be the case with the BREI so the first thing to understand is that the particular keywords that you choose are vital in locating articles that are genuinely part of your topic and for avoiding those that are not sufficiently related to your topic.

Dialog DataStar

resource.dialog.com – Advanced Search (BREI)

http://www.datastarweb.com/EDUCAT/20051017_170157_ecfce_2c/ADV8REI/2/i0d410654/

Q· Google

options   logoff   saved searches   alerts   tracker   feedback   help

databases   easy search   resource portal

Advanced Search:

British Education Index - 1975 to date (BREI)

Enter your search term(s): Search tips   ☐ Thesaurus mapping

[   ]   whole document

Information added since: [   ]   or: [none]

(YYYYMMDD)

search

☐ Documents in English ☐ Documents with abstracts

Select special search terms from the following list(s):

🔸 Publication year
🔸 BREI Thesaurus - browse headings A-D
🔸 BREI Thesaurus - browse headings E-K
🔸 BREI Thesaurus - browse headings L-P
🔸 BREI Thesaurus - browse headings Q-Z
🔸 BREI Thesaurus - enter a term
🔸 Language of publication
🔸 Publication types

Top - News & FAQS - Dialog

Figure 2.3   British Educational Index Advanced Search Window

Dial g DataStar

options   logoff   saved searches   alerts   tracker   feedback   help

databases   search page   resource portal

Titles

To view one or many selected titles scroll down the list and click the corresponding boxes. Then click display at the bottom of of the page. To view one particular document click the link above the title to display immediately.

remove duplicates   save search   print screen

Documents 1 to 11 of 11 from your search **"wyse-$.AU."** in all the available information:
Number of titles selected from other pages: 0

☐   **Select All**

☐ 1   (BREI) Link to abstract/database record
        And they all lived happily ever after? The story of a paper.
        Research Intelligence, February 2004, no. 86, p. 4-8, ISSN: 0307-9023.
        Wyse-Dominic.

☐ 2   (BREI) Link to abstract/database record
        The National Literacy Strategy: a critical review of empirical evidence.
        British Educational Research Journal, December 2003, vol. 29, no. 6, p. 903-916, ISSN: 0141-1926.
        Wyse-Dominic.

☐ 3   (BREI) Link to abstract/database record
        Circular arguments: teachers and texts.
        Changing English, March 2002, vol. 9, no. 1, p. 77-84, ISSN: 1358-684X.
        Wyse-Dominic; Jones-Russell.

☐ 4   (BREI) Link to abstract/database record
        Grammar. for writing (sic)? A critical review of empirical evidence.
        British Journal of Educational Studies, December 2001, vol. 49, no. 4, p. 411-427, ISSN: 0007-1005.
        Wyse-Dominic.

☐ 5   (BREI) Link to abstract/database record
        Felt tip pens and school councils: children's participation rights in four English schools.

Figure 2.4   British Educational Index Search for Author Name Wyse

> ## ⍓ KEY FACT
>
> The Google search engine has a different search engine called *Google Scholar*. This can be more useful than the basic Google when in the early stages of preparing for an assignment.

Search for an author's name

Before I show you how to do a keyword search let's start with a simple 'Author Name' search. Your tutor has recommended a book but all the copies are out on loan from the library. So you decide to check other things that the author has written; particularly journal articles because you know that, provided your library subscribes to the journal, you will get hold of these electronically or be able to photocopy them. If you select the advanced search button next to the British Educational Index title the first thing that you see is Figure 2.3.

Next to the 'Enter your search term(s)' box there is another box which allows you to select from a number of options including 'author(s)' (the 'i' button gives guidance on how to set out the name). If you type in the name then click the search button a list of publications by the named author appears.

> ## ★ TOP TIP
>
> Here are the steps for a simple Author Name search.
>
> 1 Access the BREI through the website of your university or college library
>
> 2 Select British Educational Index (as opposed to the Australian Education Index, or ERIC – the American version) by clicking the advanced search button
>
> 3 Select 'author(s)' in the box next to the 'Enter your search term(s)' box

4   Type in the surname (and initial if it is a common name)

5   Click 'search' button

6   Click 'Show titles' to see a list of publications

7   Decide if any of the entries are relevant to your work by clicking on the
    title of the entry and viewing immediately or by ticking the boxes and
    viewing more than one entry

8   Save any entries that are relevant to your work by selecting the format
    (e.g. PDF or text-only) then click 'save'

Let's stick to our example of the teaching and learning of grammar. If I key
in my own name, part of the displayed list of articles includes the section in
Figure 2.4.

The article called 'Grammar. for writing (sic)? A critical review of
empirical evidence' is clearly about grammar and is published in an educational journal so looks relevant.

⚷ KEY FACT

Sic ⑤ literally means 'thus'; in other words although the word might look
incorrect or questionable it is quoted exactly as it was in the original version.
(Unfortunately the BEI hasn't quite got this right because the original is 'Grammar. For Writing?' – notice the full stop after grammar and the capital F).

As I was the author of the article, I can tell you that it is about the teaching
and learning of grammar and is a high-level review of research with critical
reflections on government policy including the resource for primary teachers
called *Grammar for Writing*.

A keyword search

Now, back to a more sophisticated keyword search. If you are going to find some of the most relevant article titles you need to choose the most appropriate keywords. To help with this you can use the *Thesaurus mapping* function. Let's continue with our example: the teaching of grammar. If you tick the Thesaurus mapping box then type in the word grammar you will see a list of *descriptors*. If you click on the word 'grammar' in the list you are shown a 'tree' of folders which are called 'Special search terms'. This tree is helpful because it shows you the hierarchy of the different key words that are related to your topic of grammar.

The term 'grammar' has 761 records associated with it. This means there are 761 records that include the BREI special search term, grammar. Unfortunately that is too many records to read through efficiently so we need to limit the search. The *scope note* (which explains the key words) indicates that the term grammar is strongly associated with linguistics more than the teaching of grammar so perhaps we need to try a different term. One of the 'related terms' is 'writing skills'. The term writing skills looked promising so I selected it and then clicked the search button. The result was 293 records. It would probably take about 45 minutes to look through all those records which is still too long. The scope note for writing skills showed that another term was 'writing teaching' which also looked promising but still had 259 records.

One very useful strategy to limit your search is to combine the steps in the search history using words such as 'and', 'or' or 'not'. Each one of the items in the search history is given a number. You can combine items in the search history by simply entering numbers from the list separated by a word (such as 'and'), then click the search button: for example '1 and 4'. By doing this to link the terms 'grammar' and 'writing teaching' the number of items was reduced to eight.

★ TOP TIP

Limit your search by specifying particular years such as a range from 2003 to the present.

Eight records is certainly a manageable list to look through. The next thing to do is to check which of the items are most relevant to your work. One way to do this is to simply read the title of the article. The other way is to read the title of the journal. Quite a lot of the journals to do with grammar are about the teaching of foreign languages (such as *The International Journal of Language and Communication Disorders*) so are not relevant to our current search. For our grammar teaching example we primarily want education journals (although a journal from psychology like *The British Journal of Educational Psychology* will sometimes be relevant). Journals like *The British Educational Research Journal* or *The British Journal of Educational Studies* which have education in the title are the ones to check first. *English in Education* is an example of a subject specific journal which often focuses on implications for policy and practice.

Having located some items in the list that appear to be about the teaching of grammar the full record of any item can be viewed and then saved in the same way that I described for the author search above. The following is an example of a full record:

Accession number & update
0000132400 20050101.
Title
Principled understanding? Teaching the active and passive voice.
Source
Language and Education, 2003, vol. 17, no. 5, p. 355-370, ISSN: 0950-0782.
Author(s)
Myhill-Debra.
Descriptors
VERBS; PRIMARY-EDUCATION; GRAMMAR; CLASSROOM-COMMUNICATION; SENTENCE-STRUCTURE; CLASSROOM-ENVIRONMENT; TEACHING-METHODS.
Language
English.
Publication type
Case-Studies; Journal-Article.
Country of publication
England.

Availability
BLDSC number: 5155-694450.
Publication year
2003.
Publication date
20030000.

If you look at the 'descriptors' which are the key words for our search you will see that 'writing teaching' does not appear in this record. It was not identified by our combination of 'grammar' and 'writing teaching' because it is not linked with *both* those terms. This shows that you can miss records if you do not thoroughly explore different terms and combinations of terms.

Having done your keyword search and established a list of relevant articles your next job is to find out which ones are held by your library. By keying in the name of the journal into the library catalogue you will find this out. Usually there will be a hyperlink to the website which provides access to the journal. If not, you may have to locate the journal through a service like *Ingenta*. If your library does not subscribe to the journal then you will have to complete an *inter-library loan* ⊖ form. For a moderate charge you will then be able to have the article sent to you by the British Library but this can take as long as two weeks.

⚷ KEY FACT

An inter-library loan is a service which allows you to borrow books or receive photocopies of journal articles that are not available in your library. There is usually a small charge for each item.

The BEI is the most appropriate index for education students but there are many other search tools that work in similar ways. *Child Data* is an example that may be relevant, as this is an index of publications related to children and childhood. It includes a wider range of non peer-reviewed documents. Another index is *Books in Print* where you can search for book titles, but you need to bear in mind the things that I have said about the limitations of books to support higher-level assignments.

★ TOP TIP

Aim to limit your search until you can display 75 or fewer records.

⚕ KEY FACT

You will not be able to access a journal electronically if your library does not subscribe to the journal.

Reading and Recording

Once you have found some texts that are relevant to your writing you need to read them and record the useful information. The most effective way of doing this is to create an annotated bibliography. This can simply be a word-processed document. For each text that you read you should note the full reference information in the correct format (see Chapter 3). There are two reasons for this:

a)   If the text is a book, you may want to re-read it at some point after you have returned it to the library. You will be able to find it again easier if you have recorded the reference information;

b)   If the reference information is correctly formatted you will be able to cut and paste it to the reference list of your completed assignment.

Beneath the reference information you should record your notes about the text. You should paraphrase (put into your own words) the ideas which you think are important. You should also copy exactly some direct quotes that you might use (make sure you record the page numbers because you will need them if you are to use the quotes in your assignment). If your annotated bibliography becomes long you may find it useful to organise the document with subheadings which broadly represent the kinds of issues that are being raised by the texts that you have read. This will help later when you come to structure your writing (see Chapter 6).

I have recommended that you should read the texts and add notes to a word processed document. Unfortunately there are a minority of students who adopt a rather damaging approach to texts. At the University of Cambridge library they held an exhibition called *Marginalia and other Crimes*. This showed the extraordinary ways that some books are treated. Here is a list of the main kinds of damage:

- water

- fire

- ink

- coffee

- dogs

- mice

- children's stickers

- children's scribbling

- pigeon droppings

- pencil marks rubbed out (this always damages paper however carefully carried out)

- pencil/crayon

- highlighter pens

- adhesive notes like 'post-its' (which lift the print and/or tear the paper)

- marginal authors' who leave a signature and even an address (frequently not genuine)

- obscene comments and sometimes a response, rather like graffiti

- a series of numbers next to sentences underlined in pen to help with the points of an essay

- and worst of all ... ripping out pages or cutting out photographs which is regarded as theft. One business studies student said that they thought that if they ripped out key articles in the top journal they would have a competitive edge over their peers!

If you would like to see some photos of the damage go to http://www.lib. cam.ac.uk/marginalia/. All of these are careless and thoughtless acts which spoil subsequent readers' experiences of the texts.

When you are reading and recording your thoughts about books it is not necessary to read the whole book. If the book is an edited collection with a series of chapters by different authors then some of the chapters will be relevant to you and others will not. Other books written completely by one or more authors also do not need to be read from start to finish. You will need to use the contents and in particular the index to help you locate particular topics of interest. Skimming and scanning will also help you to skip content that is not relevant to you. However, you may find that in the early stages of your course it helps to read longer sections in full so that you gradually acquaint yourself with the particular language of your field.

Some people argue that it is possible to learn to *speed-read* ❺; if this is true then it could be a helpful technique when preparing for assignments. Tony Buzan has written a popular book on the subject (Buzan, 2003). One of the techniques to help you to remember subject matter that he describes is the 'mind-map'. This is like a spider diagram where you map the key concepts, issues and ideas. This visual representation is helpful to some people more than others. Essentially, like many such strategies, it is a summarising technique which leaves you with prompts that remind you about the issues. I was quite pleased to summarise all the key messages from his book in my simpler in *text-map*:

Conditions for Speed-Reading

1   Make sure that the time of day is good for concentration.

2   Set goals for time and amount of material to be read.

3   Activate prior knowledge of subject; remind yourself about what you know already and review easy texts on the subject.

4   Preview material first: skim and scan through entire text.

5   Read larger chunks of text than you normally would, for example three lines at a time. 'Cyclopean' and peripheral vision can be used (a claim that you can use more of your eyes' capacity than you normally do).

6   Use one of the special eye movement techniques: forwards and back-wards; zigzags; Ss; loops; wave motion running centrally down the page; margin lines.

7   Check your comprehension when you reach the end of the section you have decided to speed-read. Make some notes.

Increasing Speed

1   Use a metronome to set speed for lines read.

2   Time your progress on a chart.

3   Check your normal reading after each exercise.

4   Aim to increase your speed by 100 wpm each read.

5   Start with 2000 words in one minute then increase time to 4000 words in two minutes and so on.

6   Speed-read whole chapters.

I have tried the speed-reading techniques and have found that they work to a certain extent, particularly if I am under pressure to read a set amount. I have not particularly tried to increase my speed other than the time when I first read the book and wanted to try the techniques. One of the problems that speed-reading poses for the academic reader is that a good assignment requires close analysis of the particular words and phrases of different texts in order to appreciate the nuances of language that are part of the arguments.

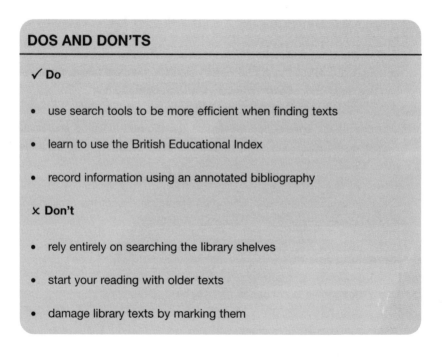

DOS AND DON'TS

✓ Do

- use search tools to be more efficient when finding texts

- learn to use the British Educational Index

- record information using an annotated bibliography

✗ Don't

- rely entirely on searching the library shelves

- start your reading with older texts

- damage library texts by marking them

3 Referencing

Referencing is an important part of any academic text. If you are able to master the conventions you will attain more marks in your course assignments. This chapter explains the *author/date system* ⓖ of referencing. Citations and references are defined and you are shown how to set out the most common kinds of references in educational texts. The chapter concludes with some notes about the *Endnote* software package.

Referencing is the process of referring to texts and ensuring that the reader has the necessary information to locate them. A reference consists of two parts:

1 The *citation* is included as part of a sentence in a text: it is signalled by an author's surname and the year of publication of their text, for example, (Wyse, 2005). A citation may or may not include a direct quote.

2 The information about the citation is located in a list, called a *reference list* ⓖ, at the end of the text which gives all the information that a reader needs if they want to read the cited texts themselves.

> ⚷ **KEY FACT**
>
> A reference list is an alphabetic list of full reference information about the texts that you have cited.

> ⚷ **KEY FACT**
>
> A *bibliography* Ⓖ is not the same as a reference list. A bibliography includes texts that you have read but not cited.

You can look at referencing in two ways:

1 A rather boring convention which must be correct in an assignment.

2 A vital aspect which influences the whole structure of the assignment.

It is true that at first glance referencing does not appear to be a terribly interesting topic. However, if you can master referencing you will have a much stronger knowledge of academic writing and will definitely write better assignments.

There are many different systems for referencing. For example, subjects in the humanities, like English literature and history, tend to use a *footnote system*. This is where you see a tiny (or *superscript*) number near a word. At the bottom of the page (or sometimes at the end of the book or article) the number will appear again next to a note which often adds further explanation.

Most education texts use the *Harvard* or *Author/Date system*. Unfortunately the description Harvard system can lead to confusion because Harvard is not one system but more a general description of a range of similar author/date referencing styles. For example, most publishers of educational books use the Harvard system but their specific guidance differs. This is also true of many education journals. Author/date system is a more helpful description which means that citations feature the author's surname followed by the year of publication.

University libraries usually offer guidance to students about referencing but this often explains the different kinds of systems that exist in the university rather than suggesting a style that you should follow. Most course handbooks also give guidance but you are sometimes left with more questions than answers.

The most important point is that whatever system you use, you must use it consistently. The easiest way to do that is to follow a system where the conventions are clearly laid down. In this chapter I will show you how to use an author/date system called the *American Psychological Association (APA) 5th style* ©. The reason I have chosen this is partly because many of the top education journals use this style. It is also very comprehensively explained in the fifth edition of the book by the APA which provides a clear set of conventions. This is important because a great deal of time and energy can be wasted arguing about the location of things like a semicolon in a reference rather than getting on with the business of writing. The other reason that the APA 5th style is growing in influence in education is because of a convenient link with a computer package which helps with referencing – more about that later in this chapter.

As you saw in Chapter 1, wide reading is the surest way to learn more and to achieve higher marks in your assessments. One part of this is the ability to methodically record the things that you have read and demonstrate this to the reader through your citations and reference list. A common question asked by many students is, how many references should I include in an assignment? In simple terms the more the better, because this shows how much reading that you have done. However, there's a bit more to it than that. An assessor can learn a lot from the *quality* of your references not just the number of them. In Chapter 1 you learned about the way that a text on an internet site differs from a book which differs from a peer-reviewed journal article. An assignment might have a relatively small number of references but all from high-level peer-reviewed journals. If you showed, through the way that you cited these texts, that you had clearly understood the articles and were able to use them effectively to enhance your writing then this would show evidence of a higher-level of learning than if you had relied mainly on internet sites. In this case your shorter reference list would be more impressive than a longer one with lower-level publications listed.

How to cite and reference

The most difficult part of referencing is getting the reference list correct. Unfortunately it is often one of the last things that you do when preparing an assignment. You may well be tired and up against a deadline and it is times like this when mistakes are often made. However, as I've explained, if you really check carefully there are benefits to getting the reference list correct for the assignment as a whole, not just for reasons of conventional correctness.

The reference list should have all items arranged alphabetically at the end of the text, formatted with hanging indents (as opposed to first line indents) and no line spaces, unless the whole text is more than single spaced. Do not have separate sections for books and journals, and so on.

★ TOP TIP

Do not include texts that you have read but have not cited in your assignment. You only do this if the assignment has a bibliography rather than a reference list.

Citations are placed within sentences. They enable you to put forward points of view which link with the texts that you are citing. Sometimes you may want to add a direct quote, where you copy word-for-word something that the author has said in their text. This is done if the point that was made by the author was particularly significant. But you should be cautious because many students have a tendency to quote directly too often. The main reason for too many direct quotes is often that the student has not fully understood the text in question so mistakenly thinks that the direct quote will be sufficient to make the point.

⚲ KEY FACT

The use of too many direct quotes is often a sign of weak writing.

If you notice too many direct quotes you may find that the draft of your writing should be viewed as an early version rather than as a final draft. Go back to the texts that you are citing and read them again. Make notes in your own words which summarise the points. Gather together the notes from related texts under *subheadings* ☺. Then redraft once more, replacing most of the direct quotes with author/date citations only.

The main reason for having a direct quote is if it is particularly important to your argument and you want to emphasise that the author of the quote has something really significant to say. Notice that a long quote of 40 or more words should be indented with author, date and page number placed either in the introductory text or immediately following the quote. You do not need quotation marks for a quote of this kind. Here's what the first part of this paragraph would look like when laid out as a long quote:

> The main reason for having a direct quote is if it is particularly important to your argument and you want to emphasise that the author of the quote has something really significant to say. Notice that a long quote of 40 or more words should be indented with author, date and page number placed either in the introductory text or immediately following the quote. (Wyse, 2006: 35)

A quote of less than 40 words should have double quotation marks and should not be indented. Single quotation marks are used for quotes within quotes. They are also used for direct speech and turns of phrase.

ᛏ KEY FACT

The grammar of the *sentence* ⓖ which includes the direct quote should make complete sense and should flow appropriately.

★ TOP TIP

Do not have too many quotes of more than 40 words. One or two in a 3500 word assignment is usually enough.

The list below shows you exactly how to set out references and write citations for the most commonly used texts in education assignments.

Book

Entry in reference list:

> Harste, J. C., Woodward, V. A., & Burke, C. L. (1984). *Language stories & literacy lessons*. Portsmouth, N. H.: Heinemann Educational Books.

Example of citation:

> Harste, Woodward and Burke (1984) investigated the language and literacy experiences of 68 children aged between three and six. Their evidence strongly emphasised the positive achievements of these children. The conclusions of the study raised some challenging questions about nursery teachers' expectations of children.

When a text has two authors always cite both names. When a text has three, four, or five authors cite all authors the first time. In subsequent citations use the surname of the first author followed by *et al.* ⓖ and the year of publication. When a text has six or more authors cite the name of the first author followed by 'et al.' All authors' names should appear in the reference list unless there are more than six names where you should provide the initials and surnames of the first six authors and shorten any others by using 'et al.'

KEY FACT

'Et al.' literally means 'and others'.

The actual year of publication should be used, *not* reprint dates. If the book is a second edition then the edition date is used and the title in the reference list will include the words *2nd edition* (or *3rd edition* and so on).

Chapter in edited book

Tizard, B. (1993). Early influences on literacy. In R. Beard (Ed.), *Teaching literacy balancing perspectives*. London: Hodder and Stoughton.

Tizard (1993) found that early learning of the alphabet and children's skill at writing their names were indicators of future reading achievement. She pointed out that although there were other indicators her research was unable to verify that they had the same influence.

Notice that the normal order for surname and initial is reversed for the editor's name, for whom the initial is first.

Journal article

Wyse, D. (2003). The national literacy strategy: a critical review of empirical evidence. *British Educational Research Journal, 29 (6)*, 903–916.

Wyse (2003) showed that the National Literacy Strategy Framework for Teaching was not adequately supported by research evidence.

You need the volume, the part number in brackets (if there is one) and the page range from the first to last page of the article.

Organisation

Department for Education and Employment (DfEE) and The Qualifications and Curriculum Authority (QCA). (1999). *The national curriculum. Handbook for primary teachers in England. Key stages 1 and 2.* Norwich: Her Majesty's Stationary Office (HMSO).

The third version of the national curriculum was written in 1999 and disseminated in 2000 (Department for Education and Skills/Qualifications and Curriculum Authority, 1999).

At the time of writing this was the correct way to reference the National Curriculum.

Newspaper

Richards, C. (1997, 24 January). Individuality, equality and discovery. *Times Educational Supplement.*

The continuing interest in the Plowden Report was revealed by a special section in the *Times Educational Supplement* which included an important article by Richards (1997).

Newspapers should not be used to strengthen your argument in the way that books and journals can. However they can be used if your focus is to analyse the way that the media writes about things and to give an indication of the current events of the time.

Report

Alexander, R., Rose, J., & Woodhead, C. (1992). *Curriculum organisation and classroom practice in primary schools: A discussion paper [the three wise men report]*. London: Department for Education and Science (DES).

Alexander, Rose and Woodhead (1992) were critical of a number of aspects of primary education including the practice of the integrated day which was also known as 'topic work'.

⚷ KEY FACT

Square brackets are used to indicate that you have added some information that is not part of a text that you are referring to.

The information in square brackets is not part of the reference but may help readers who are more familiar with the alternative name. Government departments often change their name (for example, DES, DFE, DfEE, DfES) so make sure that you have the correct version.

Film/Video

Adamson, A., & Jenson, V. (Directors) (2001). *Shrek* [Motion Picture]. In A. Warner, J. H. Williams & J. Katzenberg (Producers). United States: DreamWorks.

The humorous way that *Shrek* (Adamson and Jenson, 2001) satirises classic Disney films is at its height in the scene with the exploding bird duet.

Baddeley, G. (Ed.) (1992). Learning together through talk [Videocassette]. In Oracy Video (Producer). United Kingdom: Hodder and Stoughton.

The Baddeley (1992) video supports the pack by showing good practice in speaking and listening.

Electronic formats

> Wyse, D. (2001). Grammar. For writing? A critical review of empirical evidence [electronic version]. *British Journal of Educational Studies, 49 (4)*, 411–427.

Wyse (2001) showed that there was a lack of research evidence to support the idea that grammar teaching improves children's writing.

> Office for Standards in Education (OfSTED). (1999). A review of primary schools 1994–1998. Retrieved July 11, 2000, from http://www.officialdocuments.co.uk/document/ofsted/ped/ped.htm

The report (Office for Standards in Education, 1999) lacked the necessary rigour that was a feature of previous national inspection reports.

At a minimum, a reference to an internet source should provide a document title or description, a date (of publication and/or of retrieval), and the URL/ address (uniform resource locator). Use (n.d.) if no date of publication is available (but still include the retrieval date at an appropriate point). If you refer to multiple pages then a home page reference may be more helpful for the reader. If the author of the document is not identified then begin the reference with the title.

The internet is being used more and more as a source of reference. However, the information is usually low-level and introductory and does not go through the peer-review process. The exception to this is when peer-reviewed journal articles are replicated in electronic formats. In this case the normal journal conventions apply with the addition of the words '[Electronic version]' if you have only seen the electronic version.

Secondary source

> Wray, D., & Medwell, J. (1994). *Teaching primary English: The state of the art*. London: Routledge.

In relation to the teaching of reading the phrase 'the great debate' has been attributed to Chall (as cited in Wray and Medwell, 1994).

If you cite a text cited by someone else it is known as a secondary source. You should give the secondary source in the reference list. In the main text, name the original work and cite the secondary source. Use the author of the original text but in brackets put 'as cited in …' followed by the author(s) of the secondary source.

Do not use secondary sources unless the text is very important to your argument and it is not possible to get an inter-library loan. You should read texts yourself first-hand because the author of the secondary source may have misread the text and is likely to interpret it in a different way from yourself. You learn more by reading things yourself.

Conference presentation

Spendlove, D., & Wyse, D. (2005, 23 April). *Definitions and barriers: Perspectives on creative learning.* Paper presented at the Documenting Creative Learning symposium, University of Cambridge.

An empirically-based definition of creative learning was put forward by Spendlove and Wyse (2005).

This format is probably the most appropriate if you want to cite something from one of your lectures:

Wyse, D. (2005, 18 November). *Spelling.* Lecture presented as part of PGCE Early Years and Primary Education Course, University of Cambridge.

Laws

You do not need to include laws in your reference list, they are usually only cited in the main text. You should always include the year of the law (not in brackets) after its name.

Kenneth Baker was the education minister when the Educational Reform Act 1988 was enacted.

Classic texts

Carroll, L. (1984). *Alice's Adventures in Wonderland*. London: Gollanz. (Original work published 1863)

You can see evidence of Carroll's work as a mathematician in his classic text 'Alice in Wonderland' (Carroll, 1863/1984).

The citation should show both the original date of publication and the date of the version that you read.

Endnote

To conclude this chapter an endnote about *Endnote*! As you can see, it is not an easy task to create a perfect set of citations and references. However, further help is at hand. The computer package Endnote will do it all for you. Hmm, if only it was as simple as that. It is true that Endnote can make the task of citing and referencing much easier. In order to use it though, you need to be sure that you understand the principles of referencing that have been outlined in this chapter. Then you will need to familiarise yourself with the way that the software works. Finally you should try to use Endnote as part of your work for an assignment and learn more about how it works, by using it.

Any references that you find have to be entered into what is called the Endnote 'library'. This is a complete list of all the references that you have entered. There are three main ways to enter references. The simplest way is to use the 'new record' function as shown in Figure 3.1.

You complete the relevant categories for the kind of reference that you are entering and then as soon as the window is closed the reference is added to the library. The second way of adding references to the library is to import them from a document. The document has to be in text-only format (without any formatting) and the references have to be laid out in a particular style as shown in Figure 3.2.

Once you have got the style of the reference document ready you then simply import the file into Endnote and it adds the references to the library.

Figure 3.1   Endnote software New Record window

The third way of entering references can save you considerable amounts of time. If you have done a search on the British Educational Index (see Chapter 2) you can import the references directly in the style that they were saved in the index so you do not even need to type them yourself.

After you have entered the references the Endnote library looks like Figure 3.3.

It is now very straightforward to insert a citation and reference into your text. You select the reference in the Endnote library then position the

```
○○○                          📄 Endnote Import.txt
⌐·⅛‧‧‧‧‧‧‧¹‧‧‧‧‧‧²‧‧‧‧‧‧³‧‧‧‧‧‧⁴‧‧‧‧‧‧⁵‧‧‧‧‧‧⁶‧‧‧‧‧‧⁷‧‧‧‧‧‧⁸‧‧‧‧‧‧⁹‧‧‧‧¹⁰‧‧‧‧¹¹‧‧‧‧¹²‧‧‧‧¹³‧‧‧‧¹⁴‧‧‧‧¹⁵‧‧‧‧¹⁶‧‧‧‧¹⁷‧‧‧‧¹⁸‧‧‧

    %0 Government Report
    %A Earl, L.
    %A Fullan, M.
    %A Leithwood, K.
    %A Watson, N.
    %A Jantzi, D.
    %A Levin, B.
    %A Torrance, N.
    %D (2000)
    %T Watching and Learning: OISE/UT Evaluation of the implementation of the
    National Literacy and Numeracy Strategies.
    %C Nottingham
    %I DfEE Publications

    %0 Electronic Source
    %A Qualification and Curriculum Authority,
    %A Department for Education and Skills,
    %D 2005
    %T Schemes of Work
    %U http://www.standards.dfes.gov.uk/schemes3/

    %0 Book
    %A Wyse, D.
    %A Jones, R.
    %D (2001)
    %T Teaching, English, Language and Literacy
    %C London
    %I RoutledgeFalmer

    —
```
```
Page        Sec 1           At      Ln      Col 21      294/333      ○REC ○TRK ○EXT ○OVR
```

Figure 3.2   Text-Only format for importing references into Endnote

cursor at the place in your document where you want the citation to be placed. When you click the relevant icon Endnote inserts the citation in the correct format (depending on which format you have selected, for example, APA 5th style). If there is more than one citation with the same name and year Endnote automatically adds the appropriate letters, for example, (Wyse, 2005a), to demarcate the different references. Finally Endnote inserts the full reference in the correct place in the reference list and in the correct format. In order to make sure that I had formatted the references the correct way for the examples in this chapter I added them to my Endnote library and then used the 'copy formatted' command in the edit menu and pasted them into this chapter.

Author	Year	Title	Journal/Secondary Title
Adamson	2001	Shrek	
Alexander	1992	Curriculum Organisation and Classroom Practice in Primary Schools: A Discussion P....	
Alexander	2000	Culture and Pedagogy: International Comparisons in Primary Education	
Alexander	2004	Still no pedagogy? Principle, pragmatism and compliance in primary education	Cambridge Journal of Education
Alexander	1995	Versions of Primary Education	
Amabile	1985	Motivation and creativity: effects of motivational orientation on creative writers	Journal of Personality and Social Psychology
Amabile	1990	Within You, Without You: The Social Psychology of Creativity, and Beyond	Theories of Creativity
Applebee	1987	How writing shapes thinking: A study of teaching and learning	
Baddeley	1992	Learning Together Through Talk	
Bayliss	2003	Opening Minds: Taking Stock	
Brophy	1986	Teacher Behaviour and Student Achievement	Handbook of Research on Teaching
Bryson	1990	Mother Tongue. The English Language.	
Clarke	1976	Young Fluent Readers: What can they teach us?	
Craft	2000	Creativity Across the Primary Curriculum: Framing and developing practice	
Cropley	2001	Creativity in Education and Learning: A guide for teachers and educators	
Crystal	1997	The Cambridge Encyclopedia of Language	
Crystal	2004	Rediscover Grammar (Third Edition)	
Crystal	2004	The Stories of English	
Csikszentmih...	1990	The Domain of Creativity	Theories of Creativity
Cunningham	2002	Progressivism, decentralisation and recentralisation: local education authorities and ...	Oxford Review of Education

Showing 94 out of 94 references.

Hide Preview

Figure 3.3   Endnote library window

DOS AND DON'TS

✓ Do

- gather all necessary reference information as you carry out your background reading

- use the conventions explained in this chapter

- check that in your final draft the citations match the entries in your reference list, and that there aren't any extra references that in the end you did not cite

✗ Don't

- regard referencing as insignificant

- mix different styles of referencing

- paraphrase other people's texts (including those on the internet) without a proper citation and reference

4 Planning

One of the main differences between speech and writing is the way that writing can be planned. Careful planning is a powerful way to improve writing. In recognition that some writers prefer to plan in detail before writing whereas others just want to write first, this chapter recommends to you the idea of retrospective planning in addition to the merits of pre-planning.

All writers plan their writing. The planning may be mainly done in the head or it may be written down in great detail or more often will be a mixture of the two. When I talk about planning I mean planning that is done before you write the first draft. However, I am also going to talk about *retrospective planning* **G**. This is planning that is sharpened up after you have written the first draft. It reflects the fact that writing and planning are closely related and to a certain extent happen simultaneously.

Writers' own accounts of their planning processes show that there are considerable differences in the way this is approached. Carter (1999) collected together the thoughts of a number of fiction writers and included reflections on the routines that they used for writing. Helen Cresswell, a prolific and talented author for both children and adults, describes her way of composing:

> With most of my books I simply write a title and a sentence, and I set off and the road leads to where it finishes. All my books are like journeys or explorations. Behind my desk I used to have this saying by Leo Rosten pinned up on the wall that went 'When you don't know where a road leads, it sure as hell will take you there.' When I first read that, I thought, that's exactly it! That's what happens when I start on my books – I really don't know what's going to happen; it's quite dangerous, in a way. I often put off starting because it seems a bit scary. Yet at the end of the day, I feel that a story has gone where it's meant to have gone. (Carter, 1999: 118)

There are other writers who carry out written plans in detail before they write a word.

> Unlike novelists like Brian Moore, who write to discover what happens to their characters, Iris Murdoch writes nothing until she knows how the story will develop:
> 'I plan in enormous detail down to the last conversation before I write the first sentences. So it takes a long time to invent it.' (Harthill, 1989: 87)

It is important that you develop a style of planning that works best for you. This style is likely to be refined as you develop your writing. My view is that the more experienced you become as a writer of a particular kind of text, or genre, the less written planning you need.

⚷ KEY FACT

To many people the term 'genre' means a particular kind of fiction writing like 'romance' or 'thriller'. In education the term refers to all different types of texts such as a newspaper article or poem or speech and so on.

In the early stages of your development as a writer you need to plan by writing things down more. But as you become more experienced you can hold the equivalent of plans in your mind. Let me give an example from my own development as a writer. As part of the process of getting the contract for this book I had to write a synopsis of the content. Here is the summary I wrote for this chapter:

5. Planning

The merits of planning writing will be discussed. Suggestions will be given on possible formats for planning including keyword paragraph plans. The concept of retrospective planning will be explained and examples given. Examples of professional writers' ways of planning will be discussed.

Not much detail. But the reason I am able to write approximately 3000 words from such a basic plan is to do with my experience and knowledge as a writer. This is my seventh book, so I have a good idea about how to write non-fiction. I know the style and the structural possibilities. I am also drawing upon my extensive work with students. This knowledge helps me to think about the kind of text that I hope will be useful. My planning has not always been as minimal as this.

My first book proposal began its life as a plan represented by many sheets of A4 paper Sellotaped together and stuck onto a wall. Each sheet represented ideas about a particular section of the book. In a way it was like a very detailed contents page with notes. The main thing I learned by doing this was to summarise a complete text relatively briefly, if a whole wall can be counted as brief! This is the main job of a writing plan: to summarise your whole text. It also provides a sequence of prompts to enable you to keep your writing moving forward. Although my first book proposal was not published I learned a great deal from the process. My second proposal skipped the planning sheets on the wall stage and started with fairly detailed plans for each chapter typed into the word processor which were used for the synopsis in the proposal. This time the idea was liked by three publishers. At the time I was also getting to grips with the writing of research journal articles. For each section of the articles I wrote keywords and phrases to help me decide what to include.

Overall, my written planning is now less than it used to be. However, one of the things that I still do, as I'm writing and ideas occur to me, is add notes at the end of the text to remind me to cover particular topics and ideas. Sometimes I will use the word processor's very useful *comment* function to things that I still do, as I'm writing and ideas occur to me, is add notes at the end of the

text to remind me to cover particular topics and ideas. Sometimes I will use the word

processor's very useful 'comment' function to remind me to add something or check

something later. Figure 4.1 shows a comment set out as a speech bubble in "page layout

view". Figure 4.2 shows the comment set out in "normal view" with the "reviewing

pane" at the bottom of the window.

Insert figures 4.1 (Comment Function Of Microsoft Word In Page Layout View) and

4.2 (Comment Function Of Microsoft Word In Normal View) near here

Some people recommend the use of visual techniques to aid planning. One of the

most popular versions of this is the mind-map or topic web. I think these are most useful

in the early stages of your thinking when you are still trying to decide which areas to

4 Planning.doc

Dominic Wyse 31/7/05 11:06 AM
Comment: Here's how the comment function looks in speech bubble format

Figure 4.1   Comment function of Microsoft Word in Page Layout view

Figure 4.2   Comment function of Microsoft Word in Normal View

remind me to add something or check something later. Figure 4.1 shows a comment set out as a speech bubble in *page layout view*. Figure 4.2 shows the comment set out in *normal view* with the *reviewing pane* at the bottom of the window.

Some people recommend the use of visual techniques to aid planning. One of the most popular versions of this is the mind-map or topic web. I think these are most useful in the early stages of your thinking when you are still trying to decide which areas to include in your assignment and which areas to leave out. However, you need to go a step further than this.

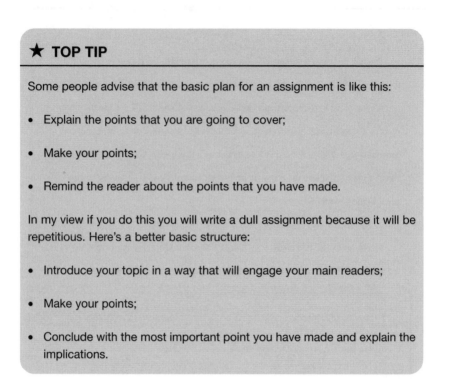

★ **TOP TIP**

Some people advise that the basic plan for an assignment is like this:

• Explain the points that you are going to cover;

• Make your points;

• Remind the reader about the points that you have made.

In my view if you do this you will write a dull assignment because it will be repetitious. Here's a better basic structure:

• Introduce your topic in a way that will engage your main readers;

• Make your points;

• Conclude with the most important point you have made and explain the implications.

As a reflection of the fact that texts are normally written in a linear way then it is my view that the most effective planning is simply a list of headings, keywords/phrases and notes. Think of it as an extended contents page without the page numbers.

Student example

A student assignment required a 2000 word comparison between two contrasting English lessons. The plan that Natasha wrote was as follows:

Introduction
My literacy lessons

Lesson 1

Lesson 2

Comparison of both lessons

Here's how Natasha's final essay looks in a retrospective plan:

℡ KEY FACT

A retrospective plan is one that is written after you have done a draft of writing. It is a way of updating early planning to check that the structure of subheadings and paragraphs are in the appropriate sequence and that you are happy with the topics that you have selected.

Comparison between a structured literacy hour lesson and a non-literacy hour lesson [title]

Paragraph 1 (P1): Key features of the NLS Framework for Teaching

P2: The segments of the literacy hour

My Literacy Lessons [sub-heading level 1]

P3: 1 sentence about weeks in the term that the two lessons were delivered

P4: Social characteristics of class

P5: Focus of the unit of work and place of lesson 1 within this

Lesson 1 [sub-heading level 2]

P6: Description of lesson 1 with focus on literacy hour structure

P7: Brief comment about restricting effect of literacy hour structure including reference to Collins and Marshall (2002)

P8: Behaviour of pupils; level of support; differentiation including for children with SEN; use of commercial scheme

(Continued)

(Continued)

Lesson 2 [sub-heading level 2]
P9: Description of lesson 2 with focus on open structure
P10: Flexibility of this lesson compared to lesson 1
P11: Response by pupils, particularly girls and pupils of different 'ability'
P12: The impact of mixed-ability groups
P13: Two sentences about lack of need for adult intervention
P14: Pupil behaviour; pupil evaluations; reference to Collins and Marshall

Comparison of both lessons [sub-heading level 2]
P15: Teacher's role 'directive' in first lesson compared to more pupil-led second lesson
P16: Quality of discussion between pupils and staff in the two lessons
P17: Second lesson a 'joy to teach' compared to first lesson; reference to Smith and Whitely (2000) about prescriptive nature of literacy hour; class teacher's comments about the literacy hour
P18: Pupil's response and the difficulties of differentiating in the first lesson; 1 sentence on teaching styles; reference to Kempe (1999) about drama; mention of visual, auditory and kinaesthetic learning (VAK); references to problems for SEN children caused by literacy hour and references to Beard (2003)
P19: Two sentence summary
P20: Concluding critical points about literacy hour
P21: Concluding points about the need for more flexibility and creativity

---

The final essay had many good features. For example the clear differences that were shown between the two lessons; the critique of the literacy hour and important points made about speaking and listening. It could have been improved further by better planning (both pre-planning and retrospective planning) and redrafting. The subheadings are an important part of a plan because they divide the assignment into major sections. It is important to get the hierarchy of these correct and if you use the word processor's auto headings this can be a helpful aid to your planning. Natasha's subheading 'Comparison of both lessons' should have been a level 1 heading (at the same level as the 'My literacy lessons' heading).

Most of the paragraphs work well but you should always be suspicious about any paragraph that is only one or two sentences; these nearly always reveal a point that is not fully developed. This was the case for Natasha's third and thirteenth paragraphs. Paragraphs 8, 14, 17 and 18 similarly failed to make their main points count, but this time because too many ideas were covered in the paragraph. As far as the overall structure was concerned it would have been better to restrict the citations (see Chapter 3) to the early paragraphs. Reflections about classroom practice could then have been covered separately.

Natasha's overall approach to the assignment was logical. In order to compare lessons it is necessary to think about them separately first, then a comparison can be made. However a higher level of thinking could have been shown if she had seen what she thought was her final draft as analysis not as finished writing. Then, the next draft of writing could have built on her writing about the separate lessons by using themes, with examples chosen from both lessons, leading to stronger points. This is what is called 'synthesis' because ideas are integrated (or synthesised) through themes.

★ TOP TIP

Although analysis is a separate mental process, writing can be seen as a way to analyse. Look at your early drafts and ask yourself if they seem to be more analysis than final draft. If they represent analysis you must rework in order to move towards clear findings and conclusions. The use of themes linked to subheadings can help to ensure that you have moved beyond analysis and description towards synthesis of significant points.

Let's look at a different way that Natasha might have planned her assignment:

- Introductory material: key issues about the teaching of English and the literacy strategy covered in peer-reviewed articles and significant books. Having written the complete draft check to ensure that there is a link between these issues and those that emerge from analysis of the two lessons.

- Introductory material: brief description of context for two lessons including general differences.

- Theme 1: teaching style – nature of interaction and pupil discussion.

- Theme 2: pupils' response and learning.

- Conclusions: reflections on the merits of the literacy hour structure compared to other ways of teaching English. Revisit at least one of the key citations from introduction. Reflect on future classroom practice.

If Natasha had planned like this then the assignment would have been clearly focused on reporting two main themes: different teaching styles in the two lessons and the different pupil responses. In a relatively short assignment of 2000 words like this one it is important not to address too many issues. This risks not covering your points in sufficient depth.

If Natasha had improved her pre-planning and in particular her retrospective planning it would probably have meant some reorganisation of her assignment rather than a great deal of new writing. Once re-planned her new draft would have covered the issues as follows:

Comparison between a structured literacy hour lesson and a non-literacy hour lesson [title]

Introductory material:
Key issues about the teaching of English and the literacy strategy covered in peer-reviewed articles and significant books. Having written the complete draft check to ensure that there is a link between these issues and those that emerge from analysis of my two lessons;
P1 to P3: Key features of the NLS Framework for Teaching including reference to books and papers to put this information in context
P4: The segments of the literacy hour
P5 to P6: Research and theory on teaching style
P7: Research and theory about pupils' response to literacy hour (this may have to be omitted if over word count)

Introductory material:
Brief description of context for two lessons including general differences;
P5: General description of lessons including the way they fitted with the unit of work.
P6: Characteristics of the pupils.

Theme 1:
Teaching Style [subheading level 1]
P7: How Natasha's role as teacher was different
P8: Opportunities for flexibility
P9: The nature of other adults' interaction
P10: Quality of discussion

Theme 2:
Pupils' Response and Learning [subheading level 1]
P11: Pupils' evaluations of the lessons
P12: Significance of drama supporting differentiation
P13: Particular difficulties for SEN children in literacy hour

(Continued)

(Continued)

Conclusions: Reflections on the merits of the literacy hour structure
compared to other ways of teaching English
P14 and P15: Critical points about the literacy hour
P16 and P17: Flexibility and creativity

I have put forward my view about the exact number and sequence of paragraphs in order to show the detailed planning that you may need to do. However, it may be that Natasha would decide on a greater number of paragraphs for some of the listed topics and fewer paragraphs for others.

You can see that proper planning of assignments leads to a better structure for the text. The structure of texts is important because it relates to your understanding of the topic that you are writing about. If you have a good structure you will not only write a better assignment, you are also likely to retain the knowledge better because a good structure supports your memory by systematically organising the knowledge.

DOS AND DON'TS

✓ **Do**

- decide how you want to plan your assignments

- use retrospective planning to check the structure and logic of the writing

- remember that what you think of as a final draft may represent analysis rather than a finished product

✕ Don't

- be afraid to deviate from your initial planning

- think that you can submit an assignment with no planning at all and expect a high mark

- forget that title and subheadings are an important part of the structure

5 Small-Scale Research Projects

Education courses often require you to carry out a piece of research and write it up for the final assessment. The writing-up is a challenge which is much harder if the research has not been appropriately planned. This chapter shows you how to plan a piece of small-scale research. It concludes with an extensive example of how one student responded to tutor feedback about his research plans.

Most education courses include a significant piece of work for the final assignment. Frequently this requires you to carry out a piece of small-scale research and write it up. It is very common for the research to involve you doing some work in a classroom and reflecting on this. In Chapter 6 I offer a structure to help you write a report of your research for an assignment (sometimes called a *dissertation* ⑥ if it is a particularly important final piece). But before you can write a good report you need to understand how to plan for and carry out a good piece of research.

It is helpful to define what we mean by research. Here is the definition which will be used during the Research Assessment Exercise which universities and other research departments take part in:

... original investigation undertaken in order to gain knowledge and understanding. It includes work of direct relevance to the needs of commerce, industry, **and** to the public and voluntary sectors; scholarship, the invention and generation of ideas, images, performances, artefacts including design, where these lead to new or substantially improved insights; and the use of existing knowledge in experimental development to produce new or substantially improved materials, devices, products and processes, including design and construction. It excludes routine testing and **routine** analysis of materials, components and processes **such as** for the maintenance of national standards, as distinct from the development of new analytical techniques. It also excludes the development of teaching materials that do not embody research. (Higher Education Funding Council for England, et al. 2005: 28, original emphases)

You may have found that a bit mind-boggling because it is defining research in all fields. However the most important sentence for our purposes is that research is "original investigation undertaken in order to gain knowledge and understanding". Research is also "planned, systematic enquiry". You plan the research that you are going to do, you carry out your plans systematically then you communicate or disseminate what you found out. Many courses require students to prepare a research plan and submit it to a tutor prior to carrying out the research. This may or may not be assessed, but whether it is or not, a plan can be an important tool to help you do a good piece of research.

Before you plan your research it is important that you do some reading (see Chapters 1 and 2). At first this reading will help you become aware of the issues in the field. It is also necessary in order to collect relevant references for your assignment. If you read research accounts these can also give you ideas for the kinds of methods that you want to use. The best research deliberately extends previous work in the field in order to create new understandings.

A good research plan will start with a rationale or reason for the research based on previous work. After the rationale the next section of a research plan is usually the research questions. Research is stimulated by questions and/or a perception that something needs to be explored. Projects also often include a set of aims and/or objectives.

★ TOP TIP

Restrict your research plan to one aim and three objectives. This will help you to focus clearly and avoid planning research that will be unmanageable.

In the following example you will notice the way that the aim and objectives are very closely linked.

Research Question: How does the UN Convention on the Rights of the Child impact on children in schools?
Aim: To explore the nature and extent of children's participation in their school.

Objectives:

- Analyse eight Year 5 and eight Year 6 children's views about participation in their school.
- Compare Year 5 and Year 6 pupils' views about participation with those of school council members.
- Reflect on observations of lessons and teachers' views in order to critically reflect on the views of pupils.

It is not always necessary to have both research questions and aims. Sometimes an introductory section which puts forward a rationale for the research, based on a reading of the literature, is sufficient to replace the research questions provided there are clear aims and objectives.

In addition to the aims, objectives and questions there are several other basic considerations that will need thought. The sample or number of participants is something that can sometimes be forgotten but it is a very important consideration for all research. The first aspect of this is the number of participants that will be involved. It is technically possible to have only one participant, something which has been done using ethnographic approaches.

For example, parents' accounts of the development of their child's reading and writing are a good example of this kind of work. Other research can require thousands of participants if it is statistical survey work. In addition to basic numbers in the sample you will also need to think about the balance in terms of gender, race and socio-economic considerations. The important thing to remember is that the sample depends on the kind of research you are doing and, like all aspects of the methodology, serves to help you meet your research objectives.

Another useful thing to include in early planning is a timetable. The detail of a timetable forces you to think about a range of decisions that will need to be made. For example if you are going to do some interviews, when and where will they take place? What do you need to do to get access to the site? How long will you spend at the site? Are you allowing enough time for ongoing analysis between your visits? Although timetables may well change once you start the research, it is helpful to give yourself an overview of how you will complete the work. The end of the timetable will include time for the writing-up of the research and a final completion date.

You will also need to plan the kinds of data collection tools and methods that you are going to use. Once again it is important to think about your objectives because the methods chosen should be the ones that are best suited to helping you to achieve them. There are many good introductory texts on research methods and, as space precludes a full account in this book, I have chosen to give an example of some of the issues to do with ethics because these are particularly important to consider when working with children.

★ TOP TIP

Look at the guidance for writing a dissertation in Chapter 6. The methods section shows a series of aspects that you should include. Most of these will need to be covered briefly in a research plan.

Ethics

One of the important dimensions of research with children is ethics. Professionally funded research with children requires that research proposals are submitted to an ethics committee. This is a committee of people who have expertise in ethical matters and who will decide if the research is appropriate to be carried out with children. Some universities even require undergraduate research proposals to be vetted by an ethics committee. There is a complex set of issues to be considered when you are thinking about the ethics of your research.

Children have rights of their own which are complemented by general human rights legislation. The UN Convention on the Rights of the Child ensures that children have a right to participate in all matters that affect them. This means that if you are doing research with children they must give their own consent. In order to give their consent they must understand as much as possible about the research as appropriate to their stage of development.

For example you can say things like: 'The research I would like to do is about … you do not have to take part if you don't want to and you will not be in trouble if you decide not to take part … you can stop doing the research at any time … the only people who will know your real name as part of the research will be the researcher and the researcher's teacher (their tutor) …'

Schools can be a particularly difficult place for children to exercise consent. Too often teachers, who under the law are in *loco parentis* (which means they can take decisions as if they were a parent), sometimes oblige children to help with research without really asking for their consent. This can put you as the researcher in a tricky position because it is your duty to make sure that you have informed consent from the children. Gaining consent is particularly challenging with young children because of their general level of understanding but even nursery children can understand a straightforward explanation about the research that you are doing and can be asked if they would like to take part. You can also explain to them that they are not going to be in trouble if they don't want to be involved and that they can withdraw at any time during the research. Parental consent is also necessary for research with children.

Confidentiality is another important ethical issue. All names should be fictionalised in any written reports. You should be honest and clear with the children about who is going to know their views. As a student, yourself and your supervisor will know about the children's views. Technically it might be possible to anonymise your data to the extent that even your supervisor does not know the names of the participants but this is probably not necessary provided it is made clear to the participants. For undergraduate research it is usually better if all data are destroyed once the research is complete. At the very least data should be kept safely and securely so that any promises about confidentiality are not breached.

Research carried out by professional researchers that looks at 'controversial' topics like abuse or discrimination or which involves children with special needs always requires particularly careful thought. People who have carried out studies about abuse have recognised that the conversations that are held during interviews can lead to further trauma because of the memories that are stirred. Researchers in these situations need to be trained in counselling or should have organised professional support for those participants who might need it. It is also possible that children might disclose information about being abused which would require the researcher to contact the local social services department. In this case confidentiality cannot be maintained and written agreements with older children make this clear. Child abuse is not a suitable topic for inexperienced researchers and you should take advice from tutors if thinking about other kinds of research in controversial areas.

Strong arguments have been presented which suggest that research that is ethically appropriate should result in demonstrable benefits to children. One way of achieving this is by involving the children themselves in the research. The highest level of involvement comes when children carry out the research themselves from planning to finished product. However, the supervision of such work requires a high level of skill and knowledge of the research process and knowledge of how children might work within such a process. Lower levels of involvement are possible. Kirby (1999: 46) suggests that for the different stages in the research process six levels of involvement by children can be considered:

- None

- Be informed

- Express a view

- Influence a decision

- Be a partner in a decision

- Be the main decision-maker

When you are planning your research you should have reasons for your decisions about the level of involvement from the children.

Alderson (1995: 2) presents a useful list of ethical topics – accompanied by sets of key questions – that need consideration when carrying out research with children:

1 The purpose of the research

2 Costs and hoped-for benefits

3 Privacy and confidentiality

4 Selection, inclusion and exclusion of participants

5 Funding

6 Review and revision of the research aims and methods

7 Information for children, parents and other carers

8 Consent

9 Dissemination

10 Impact on children

The best research takes account of all the items on this list (with the exception of number five for research which is not funded). There are always potential benefits and potential costs for participants in research. Apart from health and safety considerations costs can include time, inconvenience, embarrassment, intrusion of privacy, sense of failure or coercion. Benefits could include satisfaction, increased confidence or knowledge, and time to talk to an attentive listener. When you undertake research ensure that it is well planned, systematically carried out and ethically appropriate. If this is done there are benefits for participants and researchers.

Student example

It is rarely possible for tutors to closely annotate students' research plans because this is very time consuming and they have to deal with many students. This is something that in the past I have tried but found that arranging a meeting with students and discussing hard copies of their draft proposals face-to-face was more efficient. To conclude this chapter I offer the follow-ing example of a student's research plan which I *was* able to annotate. The students were given a simple list of headings that, as a minimum, they should cover in their research plan:

- Research Question(s), aim, and objectives.

- Sample/Participants

- Access

- Timetable

- Data Collection Methods

- Ethical Considerations

When you do the final writing-up for a piece of research there are many more sections that you need (see Chapter 6). A research plan is much more basic: you need to show the methods that you are going to use in order to work out that the research is feasible. At this stage you are not usually required to write a lengthy rationale which includes references, but this will be required in the form of a literature review in the dissertation.

In the boxes below you can see how one student approached the task of the research plan. The comments in bold are my responses to the first draft of his plan (although the comments are mainly criticisms, there are many positive features about this draft which I communicated to the student in the message of my email).

First Draft

Research Question(s)

(a) Does the target group agree with recent literature and media suggesting that there is more pressure on young people nowadays to achieve academically well in exams?

(b) What effects do SATs have upon the children and their teachers? i.e. child's self esteem and opinion of schooling, the teaching methods demonstrated in the classroom (teaching towards passing a specific exam rather than teaching children what they need to know about a particular subject). Increased pressure upon teachers to gain good results from their pupils – what effect does this have?

(c) How does the education system differ as a whole, nowadays to before the introduction of SAT's **(no apostrophe)**, and what impact does this have upon the concept of childhood? i.e. children have less time to experience the freedom of being a child, lack of play, pressure and focus on academic achievement – possible effects?

(d) Is the early introduction of education into a child's life an advantage – discuss different education systems with good and bad points, for example, some European countries don't start children at school until 7-years-old. **(These questions are too broad)**

Aim

To identify and discuss the opinions of 12-year-old children who have experienced the implications of early exams in their education, and

---

(Continued)

compare these findings to the recent literature and media texts **(see below)** regarding this issue.

Research Objectives

(a) To gather and analyse the views of 12-year-old children who have completed SAT's and the views of their teachers, headteacher, and if possible an examiner.
(b) To compare these views to what the literature and media texts suggest about early exams in a child's education **(this is not really an objective because it is a normal part of all research)**.
(c) To examine the impact of these exams upon the children, their teachers and possibly their parents, the education system, and the concept of 'childhood' as a whole. **(Limit this to children and teachers?)**

Methodology

Sample/Participants
I wish to carry out my research project with 20 pupils, if possible 10 boys and 10 girls. I would also like to include 2 teachers – 1 male and 1 female, the headteacher and an examiner **(how will you get access to a test examiner?)**. Depending on the results of these findings, I may also speak to some of the parents **(No uncertainty please. I would suggest leaving the parents or balancing the numbers of participants from each group)** and discuss whether they feel under more pressure to tutor their children at home from an early age due to the ever-changing education system.

Access

I have good communication links with my old high school so if my research topic is approved I should be able to use this school, and the

(Continued)

(Continued)

pupils and teachers to help me throughout the duration of my research study **(but the tests are done in primary school. Perhaps you are planning to study the tests for 14-year-olds?).**

Timetable

Yet to be completed. **(I need to see this)**

Data Collection Methods

I wish to carry out individual informal interviews with a few children – 4 or 5 – in my target group to gather their own opinions about SAT's, and possibly include a brainstorming discussion with the whole group about the effects that their exams had on them **(I like this combination of individual and group interviews)**. This will be useful as they can bounce their ideas off each other, and I will gain a more in-depth insight into their true thoughts. I would also like to give each child a questionnaire to complete using facial scale assessment **(necessary for 12-year-olds?)** and open-ended questions. I think these will be useful as the pupils may find it easier to express their comments and ideas about a certain aspect of the SAT's process, rather than if I was to talk to them face-to-face.

When researching the opinions of the adults involved in this study I wish to interview them separately to gain a different perspective on SAT's and their possible effects on children and teachers.

Ethical Considerations

Before completing the collection of this data, I will ensure that each participant is fully aware that the information given to me will be kept strictly confidential, and my study will not be used as a public document. They must also have signed a consent or assent form to show that they understand the aims of my research, and know that they have permission to leave the study process at any time. My target group has

(Continued)

been chosen so as not to discriminate against any individual, with an equal number of boys and girls, and male and female teachers.

The first draft usefully raised some issues to think about. One of the most important of these was about the scale of the research. You will find that you get excited by issues that you want to research. But often these early ideas are too broad for the kind of small-scale research that you are able to do. You need to really focus on a small manageable area. Students sometimes think that this might be boring but on the contrary, research which is tight and well focused is more interesting because the tutor and the student learn from a more rigorous exploration. Part of my advice in relation to manageability was to suggest a smaller sample. Although David thought about this, in the end he decided to stick with his idea of interviewing parents in addition to the other participants.

Another of my comments was about the style of writing. Although a research proposal requires you to speculate about how you are going to carry out your research you have to make a firm decision about what you are going to do. Some students include language such as 'I may decide to ...' It is better if the writing reads like a definite plan, even knowing that the tutor may suggest further changes.

For the second draft I was conscious of the approaching deadline for the proposals so decided to use the reviewing function of the word processor which includes *track changes*. In the example below, the boxes/bubbles in the right margin show the text which I suggest for deletion. Text that is underlined is my suggested replacement.

⚕ KEY FACT

The word processor function *Track Changes* allows any changes to a document to be shown in a different colour. It is particularly useful for writers who are collaborating. Once the changes have been seen the function can be turned off and the text shows the changed version.

2nd Draft

Title of Research: The impact of statutory tests upon young people, parents and teachers, and the concept of childhood.

Research Question (s)

(a) Does the target group agree with recent literature, suggesting that there is more pressure on young people nowadays to achieve academically in exams?

Aim

Assess the impact of statutory testing on 12-year-old children,

Research Objectives

(a) Analyse the views of a sample of children, teachers and parents about statutory testing, (b) Consider children's parents' and teachers' views about the appropriateness of assessing children from an early age.

c) Relate the views of children, parents and teachers to theoretical concepts of childhood,

Methodology

Sample/Participants

I have decided to carry out my research project with 6 12-year-old pupils 6 parents, and 6 teachers [who have had experience of teaching in preparation for the statutory tests at 11?], The groups will be balanced for gender [and ethnicity?] They will also be unrelated groups so that I can collate a variation of individual perspectives on this subject.

Access

I have good communication links with my old high school so if my research topic is approved I should be able to use this school to talk to the pupils of the sample group.

As I only want to gather general opinions from teacher's viewpoints, I will also speak to some of the teachers at this school. The remainder of my participants will come from a primary school with which I carried out a pre-teaching

Deleted: and media

Deleted: well

Deleted: -

Deleted: To identify and discuss the opinions of 12-year-old children who have experienced the implications of early exams in their education, and to associate these findings to the impact made on the concept of "childhood".

Deleted: To gather and analyse the views of 12-year-old children who have completed statutory tests, and collect general opinions from teachers and parents, on whether they agree with assessing children from an early age. ¶

Deleted: To examine the impact of these exams upon children, teachers, parents, and the concept of "childhood".

Deleted: and 6 parents

Deleted: These groups will represent an equal number of both sexes and a broad variety of ages so as not to discriminate against any participant.¶

Deleted: .

course. These teachers will be especially useful, as they have had first-hand experience of educating children of this age towards the statutory tests at 11-years-old. This bit needs reworking – which primary schools will you use?

I have easy access to many parents in my local area as I regularly baby-sit for some children, and I can interview the parents of my friends – two of which I understand to have a teaching background.

Timetable [included in this draft but to avoid repetition only shown below in draft three]

Data Collection Methods

I wish to carry out individual informal interviews with the children in my sample group to gather their own opinions about statutory tests, and the effects that they may have had. I will also include a brainstorming discussion with the whole of this group about various definitions of statutory tests. This will be useful as they can bounce their ideas off each other, and I will gain a more in-depth insight into their true thoughts.

I would also like to give each child a questionnaire to complete using multiple choice and open-ended questions. I think these will be useful as the pupils may find it easier to express their comments and ideas about a certain aspect of the assessment process, rather than if I was to talk to them face-to-face.

When researching the opinions of the adults involved in this study I wish to interview them separately to gain a different perspective on statutory tests. I will include what they believe to be the possible effects on themselves – depending on what viewpoint they take – children, and the concept of "childhood".

Ethical Considerations

Before completing the collection of this data, I will ensure that each participant is fully aware that the information given to me will be kept strictly confidential, and my study will not be used as a public document. They must also have signed a consent or assent form to show that they understand the aims of my research, and know that they have permission to leave the study process at any time. My target group has been chosen so as not to discriminate against any individual, with an equal number of male and female participants, and a broad variation of ages.

Figure 5.1   Student research proposal example showing tutor suggestions with 'track changes'

The final draft which was used as the plan for the research is below.

Final Draft

Title of Research: The impact of statutory tests upon young people, parents and teachers, and the concept of childhood.

Research Question(s)

(a) Does the target group agree with the recent literature suggesting that there is more pressure on young people nowadays to achieve academically in exams?

(b) What effects do statutory tests have upon the children and their teachers?

Aim

To identify and discuss the implications of statutory testing on 12-year-old children.

Research Objectives

(a) To gather and analyse the views of a sample of children, teachers and parents about statutory testing.

(b) To consider these views in relation to the appropriateness of assessing children from an early age.

(c) To relate the views of children, parents and teachers to theoretical concepts of childhood.

Methodology

Sample/Participants
The sample will consist of 6 pupils, 6 parents, and 6 teachers who have had experience of teaching in preparation for the statutory tests at 11. These groups will represent an equal balance of gender, ethnicity, and a broad variety of ages so as not to discriminate against any participant.

They will also be unrelated groups so that I can collate a variation of individual perspectives on this subject.

Access

I have good communication links with my old high school so if my research topic is approved I should be able to use this school to talk to the pupils of the sample group.

As I only want to gather general opinions from teachers' viewpoints, I will also speak to some of the teachers at this school. The remainder of my participants will come from a local primary school with which I carried out a pre-teaching course. These teachers will be especially useful, as they have had first-hand experience of educating children of this age towards the statutory tests at 11-years-old.

I have easy access to many parents in my local area as I regularly baby-sit for some children, and I can interview the parents of my friends – two of which I understand to have a teaching background.

Timetable

Timetable of Independent Study Process

DATE	ACTIVITY/RESEARCH TO BE UNDERTAKEN
Semester 1	
Week 4	Draft proposal. First meeting with personal tutor.
Week 5	Finish typing up proposal. Do rough drafts of outline interviews and questionnaires.
Week 6	Complete ethics form, outline of interviews and questionnaires. Alter consent and assent forms and letter of introduction. Hand in proposal to office.
Week 7	Write to schools and participants asking for permission to carry out research study if approved by the ethics committee.

(Continued)

(Continued)	
Weeks 8–11	Collect relevant sources in the form of books, journals, website addresses and newspaper/magazine articles to make reference to in dissertation.
Week 12	Decision from ethics committee is finalised. Make contact with personal tutor to check progress, and if approved collect more relevant information.
Week 13	First visit to school – carry out interviews and group discussion with pupils. Hand out questionnaires for them to complete.
Week 14 and 15	Contact personal tutor to discuss findings. Begin to analyse pupils responses to the interviews/question naires in relation to the references gathered.
CHRISTMAS BREAK	Carry out interviews with parents. Second visit to high school sometime in January to talk to some of the teachers about their opinions on the subject. Start analysis of these findings.
Semester 2	
Week 1	Make contact with primary school, and carry out visit to speak to a few of the teachers about their experiences of statutory tests, from a teacher's perspective. Talk to personal tutor about findings.
Weeks 2–4	Complete analysis of all responses to interviews and questionnaires in relation to academic texts gathered. Make contact with tutor to check progress.
Weeks 5–7	More data collection from references to validate research study.
Week 8	Begin write-up of dissertation. Contact personal tutor to make sure I'm on the right track and discuss any problems which may have arisen.
EASTER BREAK	Complete introduction and part of the main bulk of the study. Aim to write approx. 5,000–6,000 words.
Week 9	Make contact with tutor to discuss what I have completed so far. Continue with write-up.

Weeks 10–11	Complete writing up the dissertation including conclusion, bibliography, reference list, contents page and appendix. Make contact with personal tutor to discuss progress, and any problems.
Week 12	Proofreading, grammar and spellchecks of dissertation, bind together and hand in on the 7th May before mid-day!!

Data Collection Methods

I wish to carry out individual informal interviews with the children in my sample group to gather their own opinions about statutory tests, and the effects that they may have had. I will also include a brainstorming discussion with the whole of this group about various definitions of statutory tests. This will be useful as they can bounce their ideas off each other, and I will gain a more in-depth insight into their true thoughts.

I would also like to give each child a questionnaire to complete using multiple choice and open-ended questions. I think these will be useful as the pupils may find it easier to express their comments and ideas about a certain aspect of the assessment process, rather than if I was to talk to them face-to-face.

When researching the opinions of the adults involved in this study I wish to interview them separately to gain a different perspective on statutory tests. I will include what they believe to be the possible effects on themselves – depending on what viewpoint they take – children, and the concept of 'childhood'.

Ethical Considerations

Before completing the collection of this data, I will ensure that each participant is fully aware that the information given to me will be kept

(Continued)

(Continued)

strictly confidential, and my study will not be used as a public document. They must also have signed a consent or assent form to show that they understand the aims of my research, and know that they have permission to leave the study process at any time. My target group has been chosen so as not to discriminate against any individual, with an equal number of male and female participants, and a broad variation of ages.

David carried out a good piece of research and was awarded a BA (Hons.) Childhood Studies class 2.1 for his final degree with the dissertation counting strongly towards this. He took up a place on a postgraduate teacher-training course.

DOS AND DON'TS

✓ Do

- plan your research carefully because it can avoid many problems later on

- read basic research methods texts to familiarise yourself with the research process

- think carefully about the ethics of working with children

✗ Don't

- forget the importance of a realistic timetable for your research

- worry if after careful planning the research doesn't go exactly to plan

- underestimate the time required for analysis of data

Part II Writing

6 Structuring your Writing

After reading this chapter you will understand better how to structure academic writing. You will know about the typical sections to include in a dissertation and their word lengths. You will be able to use this information to support the writing of other assignments.

The overall structure of a piece of writing is revealed by the following things:

- the amount of words;

- the title;

- chapters – if the text is suitably long;

- subheadings and sections;

- paragraphs;

- general layout features.

The amount of words for a text is one important feature of the structure. It is possible to write about a topic in 100 words, 1000 words, 10,000 words or 100,000 words. A piece of 100,000 words is book length and requires chapters. A piece of 100 words is abstract length (like the summary paragraph at the beginning of this chapter) and may or may not require paragraphs.

⚷ KEY FACT

One page of text at font size 12 is about 500 words. If it is double-spaced then two pages equals 500 words.

You might think that the first thing that should be written is the title but this is not always the case. The title needs to succinctly, and at times imaginatively, sum up the whole text but this can be quite difficult to decide until the whole text has been written.

★ TOP TIP

Leave the title until you've finished writing the whole text.

Subheadings and sections

Subheadings are used to divide the text into large sections. Like the title, the subheading should clearly sum up the content of the section. Too few subheadings can make it more difficult for you to communicate the flow of your argument to the reader. Only very skilful writers can maintain clarity in long pieces without subheadings (stories are different to academic texts in this respect because the narrative of the story maintains the flow). However, too many subheadings can break the flow of your writing which can distract the reader from your intended meaning. Remember that the marker of your writing will often be reading quickly; good use of subheadings can help them understand your points quicker and more clearly which can lead to a better impression.

★ TOP TIP

On average for a 3000 word essay try at least one subheading per 500 words.

A subheading is the title for a section; a section is built from paragraphs. Quite a lot of students struggle with paragraph structure. First of all you need to understand what a paragraph is and how it works. A paragraph is a block of text which consists of a number of sentences about a particular topic. The first sentence of a paragraph is often referred to as the 'topic sentence' because it reveals to the reader what the topic of the paragraph is about.

★ TOP TIP

It is very rare to have a paragraph of only one sentence – if you spot one, check to see if the sentence would be better joined to the paragraph before or after.

If you are using a word processor it is a good idea to use the automatic *heading styles* for your subheadings. The reason for using these, rather than creating your own formatting for subheadings, is that the word processor recognises them and makes them part of the *document map*. The document map looks a bit like a contents page (and for long texts it can actually create a contents page for you, complete with the correct page numbers). If you click on the document map icon all the headings in your document are revealed in a left margin. If you click on any of the headings the cursor jumps to that section of the text. The document map is very helpful because it enables you to think about the order, number and hierarchy of your headings and sections – in other words the overall structure of your writing. The simplest hierarchy is to have the title of your writing at the level of 'heading 1' and the subheadings all at the level of 'heading 2'. If some sections are subsets of other sections then you will need to use 'heading 3', and so on.

The paragraphs in a sub-headed section represent a sequence of ideas that you are putting forward. They must have a logical order to them. The last sentence of one paragraph leads the reader into the topic sentence of the next paragraph. However, this flow of ideas is subtle. It is not that you need to *explicitly* make links between paragraphs. It is more that the careful placement of paragraphs and use of sentences will result in the logical order and satisfactory flow of ideas.

Writing a research report

Assessments which ask you to carry out observations and/or a piece of research in the classroom and then write this up are common to many courses. It is common for a course to have a final assessment like this which is sometimes called a dissertation.

⚷ KEY FACT

A dissertation is an extended piece of formal writing which explores a topic in depth and is usually based upon original research. The term is related to the word 'discourse'.

A dissertation of this sort is basically a research report. In this chapter I am going to concentrate on how to structure a good research report because it is one of the most challenging and important pieces of writing that you are likely to do. The structure of a research report is not the same as the structure of some other kinds of assessments such as lesson planning; presentations; evaluations and so on. However, if you can structure a research report really well you will find that you will also be better equipped to tackle other kinds of writing because much of the knowledge and skills can be transferred.

The purpose of a research report is to tell the reader how you carried out your research and what you found out. Often some of the writing for the report is drafted while you are still collecting the data. This sometimes results in students mistakenly using future tense (for example, 'I will be keeping a research diary') but the whole report should be past tense ('I kept a research diary') because ultimately you are reporting something that has been done in the past, once you have finished the research.

Academic writing has a particular formal style. Every word is important so you have to use language very carefully. Avoid using language which is too informal, like the kinds of phrases that you might use when speaking, innit! At the same time your use of language should be direct and clear; there is no need to use complicated language or 'big words' for the sake of it.

★ TOP TIP

Avoid the kind of informal language that these students used.
Informal: 'As part of our topic on insects we are going to *do the park*'.
Formal: 'As part of our topic on insects we are going to visit the park'.

Informal: 'The children *absolutely loved* this book'.
Formal: 'The children really enjoyed *Burglar Bill*'.

You need to be careful about making claims about your research which cannot be supported by your data and their analysis. Phrases such as

'my research found some evidence that ...' or
'it is possible that ...';

'although my findings revealed ... other studies have shown a different picture ...'

are often suitable for the discussion section because they are tentative and they show that you understand that your findings are limited to the data you acquired. Your points should be based on evidence (only from your own research data and from published research) not your personal opinions. Personal opinions are sometimes called *anecdotal evidence* **G**.

ᛦ KEY FACT

Anecdotal evidence is the information that we gather in our daily lives that informs our beliefs about the world. It is not the same as evidence that is gathered as part of research.

Some people say that you should not put forward your own point of view in a piece of academic writing. This is not accurate. A good piece of academic writing does clearly put forward the writer's view about the subject; the key thing is that the writer also considers a range of evidence that offers different perspectives to their own.

Beginning a piece of writing can often be the hardest part. Although careful planning and thinking are important there comes a point when you must start writing. Do not worry too much about getting the words exactly right at first. You will find that much of the early draft will be changed anyway. Some students put the subheading 'introduction' right at the beginning of their text. I would advise you not to do this. The introduction is simply the sentences and paragraphs at the beginning of your text. Yes, you have to choose opening sentences and paragraphs carefully so that they do sound like the beginning but there is no need for a separate introduction complete with subheading (only very long texts such as books need a separate introduction of this kind).

> ★ **TOP TIP**
>
> Start the first draft of your writing then delete some early sentences (or even paragraphs) in favour of a sentence later on that is more appropriate to begin your piece.

A suggested structure for a dissertation or research report

There are four main sections that you would expect to see in a good research report:

1 Literature Review

2 Methodology

3 Findings/Results

4 Discussion

Literature review – a review of texts related to your research topic

Not to be confused with book/film reviews in the media; an academic literature review shows that you have read widely about your topic.

- Introduce your topic of study.

- If your topic is one that is currently featured in the media this can be a moment to link with this. In general though, references to newspaper sources are not academically rigorous so do not support your arguments (see Chapter 1).

- Sometimes it can help to include personal reasons for choosing the area of study. For example experiences that you had while on school experience, or previous research that you have done. This is a rare occasion when anecdotal comment is appropriate.

- Theoretical perspectives are necessary to put your dissertation into a wider context and to achieve the highest marks. *Theory* ❻ is difficult to define because it varies so much. Some theories are short and to the point: for example, women make better drivers than men. Other theories are long and complex.

✆ KEY FACT

Theory can be defined as ideas which explain and summarise things. In research, theory is developed or confirmed by observation and experiment.

Most publications related to your topic will include some theory. Identify sections which emphasise theory, rather than research and/or practice, during your reading. Organise the key theoretical ideas as a basis for some paragraphs in your literature review.

- Define the key ideas and terms that you will use throughout the report by citing researchers' definitions published in articles. Be careful about standard dictionary definitions because some technical words can have a different meaning from the one used in everyday life (although dictionaries like the *Oxford English Dictionary* do include technical meanings of words). For example, the word 'genre' refers to different kinds of novels (like crime or romance) in everyday life, but in education it has been defined as broadly as 'the structural features of any specific spoken or written act'.

- Show that you are aware of the most recent research that is as closely related to your own as possible. Show that you have a wide knowledge of the field by making reference to some key older texts (seminal texts) that are still regarded as important.

Organise the literature review by using subheadings. When you read a selection of texts you usually find that there are some key topics that keep cropping up. Choose some of these topics as the basis of the sections of your literature review.

Example of subheadings from a student's children's literature essay:

Reasons for Choice of Roald Dahl

Sociological Aspect of Children's Literature

Historical Events

Roald Dahl – His Life

Book Analyses

Other Authors

Methodology – an account of the methods that you used and reflections on their effectiveness

The methodology needs to do three things for each of the sections below:

1 Clearly explain the methods that you used;

2 Show a deeper level of understanding of methodology by citing research methods texts;

3 Show your awareness of the strengths and weaknesses of the methods that you used in your research. Some of this awareness can be shown by a combination of 1 and 2.

- Theory – there are theories about your topic but there are also theories about methodology, for example, are you collecting mainly quantitative or qualitative data? Why? The answer to the question lies in methodological theory and its link with your objectives. Once again theoretical exploration will help you gain the highest marks.

- Research Questions/Aim/Objectives – clear aims and objectives are vital because they should be the anchor for the whole study. Research questions *and* aims may not both be needed because they are somewhat interchangeable.

★ TOP TIP

Limit yourself to one aim and three objectives which link with your research questions.

- Sample and site(s) – Give straightforward details about the participants in your research. The most basic and essential information is the number of people involved. A table can usefully set out the following information: fictional name; gender; age; ethnic origin. If the site is a school then the type of school (infant; primary) and information such as numbers of free school meals; numbers of minority ethnic pupils; and location (for example, inner-city; rural) are helpful. You should also explain how you were able to access the school.

- Ethics – statements about ethics have become much more important in recent years particularly in research with children. The main aspects of this are:

  (i)   separate informed consent by children, parents and other participants;
  (ii) the right to withdraw from research without prejudice;

(iii)   confidentiality, unless there is a duty to report (for example in the case of a disclosure about child abuse);

(iv)   the extent to which the research is in the best interests of children;

(v)   special care when working with disadvantaged groups.

- Fieldwork – a timetable showing the dates of visits, observations, interviews, and so on. Reflections on the research work that was carried out and any issues that arose.

- Data-collection methods – the methods that were used to collect data.

- Analysis – a short account of how the data were organised and analysed.

- Validity – what techniques did you use to ensure your study was valid?

In the methodology section you should cite research methods texts not texts about the topic of study (sometimes called the 'substantive area').

Findings/Results – a report of the most significant things that you found

There is some debate about the difference between findings and analysis. Analysis is something that you do by working with your data. It is something that is done largely in the mind by working on the data. Having carried out this analysis you should be in a position to report a series of findings. Often students think that they have produced findings when actually their first draft represents analysis.

★ TOP TIP

Think of early writing drafts of the findings section as a tool for analysing your data, rather than finished writing.

Remember you cannot have valid findings without rigorous, systematic and exhaustive analysis.

Following analysis you must *select* the most significant findings. To do this you need to decide which information is most important and which information you will not report. There are many possibilities for presentation:

- The use of subheadings which represent substantial categories that emerged during your analysis is often the best way to report findings.

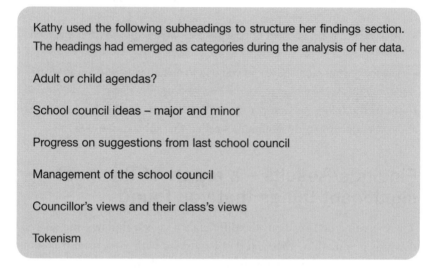

Kathy used the following subheadings to structure her findings section. The headings had emerged as categories during the analysis of her data.

Adult or child agendas?

School council ideas – major and minor

Progress on suggestions from last school council

Management of the school council

Councillor's views and their class's views

Tokenism

- Case studies of particular participants and/or sites and so on can form the main basis of the findings or can enhance other forms of presentation.

- Chronological accounts – these may be useful if the sequence of time was an important feature of the research, perhaps if you were using a diary to track your development during a teaching practice.

- Graphical representation – many people find the use of diagrams and tables to sum up findings helpful.

> ★ **TOP TIP**
>
> Tables are useful for summarising text-based data as well as numbers-based data.

- Presentation organised in order of data collection methods. This can be too simplistic and often represents analysis more than findings.

- Using different written genres – requires great confidence, and skill. Poetry and drama have been used to report research! I once presented the findings of a study about 10 teachers' English teaching as a play. One of the findings of the research was that the teachers felt inhibited by the OfSTED inspection regime and most unsure about the coherence of the policies. A chief inspector was portrayed as a babbling, incoherent, drunkard character in the play in order to stimulate debate about this finding.

The findings section should not normally include citations unless the whole study is an analysis of texts. The findings are presented in your own words.

Discussion – the implications of the research project

This is often a difficult section to write. However, if it proves to be extremely difficult it may be that you have not analysed your data deeply enough. If so go back to your analysis and findings.

Some people explicitly return to their research objectives at this point. While it is true that the whole report should be clearly related to your objectives this often works better if it is implicit in the writing. However, the restatement of objectives and reflections on how well you met them does clearly signal to the person marking the assignment that you have thought about this. The discussion section should include the following:

- Main findings – a bulleted summary perhaps.

- Short discussion about the one overall finding of the study and what you conclude from this. If space permits, a short discussion about one or more of your other main findings without repeating information in the findings section.

- Implications of your research – how might your conclusions be acted on by the participants in the study? What impact does the research have on your future thinking and practice? Can the conclusions be tentatively related to a wider perspective, for example possible impact on practice and other people's lives; links with the broader society?

- Revisit one or two key studies from the literature review and write about how you now view them in the light of having done your research.

- Optional reflections on limitations of the study. Although this is traditional it is often better covered within the methodology section.

- Recommendations are made for future research.

Abstract – summary of complete text

The abstract is actually the first section of a research report coming straight after the title. It can only be written after you have finished the whole report. The abstract is a challenge because it requires you to summarise the whole report in very few words. All four main sections of the report have to be covered in just a few sentences each.

Many students ask for guidance on how long the different sections should be. Tables 6.1 and 6.2 offer some suggestions.

These percentages can be applied to reports of different sizes. Table 6.2 shows the word-lengths for a 6000 word dissertation.

Remember, the figures are not exact, so you can have more or fewer words in each section, but they do give a general indication of the weighting of the different sections of a research report.

Table 6.1 Recommended lengths for different sections of research report expressed as percentages

Abstract	2.5% of total word-count
Literature Review	30% (Introduction 5% of this)
Methodology	17.5%
Findings	30%
Discussion	20%

Table 6.2 Recommended lengths for different sections of a 6000 word research report expressed as number of words

Abstract	150 words
Literature Review	1800
Methodology	1050
Findings	1800
Discussion	1200

Student example

To conclude the chapter we look at Jean's assignment which was to write a 500 word report about some observations that she had made of two children while on school placement. The structure of her first draft is shown in Table 6.3.

The first sentence and paragraph of any piece of work are very important because the reader quickly forms judgements about your writing at the beginning. Jean's idea to explain the way that the observations were carried out was a good one although she might have improved this with a previous introductory paragraph about some published classroom observation work that she had read. Even in a very short piece like this you can see that the idea of literature review is relevant, even if it is only one paragraph.

The phrase "For this assignment" was a weak start because it did not positively signal what the paragraph was about. It also sounded as though it was the kind of sentence that you might have half way through a paragraph rather than at the beginning. A more direct opening sentence might have

Table 6.3 The structure of the opening of the first draft of Jean's assignment

Paragraph	Topic of paragraph	First (topic) sentence
1	Information about observation process	"For this assignment we had to carry out ongoing observations of two different children ..."
2	Age of children; characteristics of Child A; characteristics of Child B	"The children who were being observed were in Year 1, age five."
3	Target-setting	"For this assignment, targets were set with the class teacher ..."

been: 'During my first placement I recorded observations of two children in the Year 1 class where I was working. The observations were carried out for 10 minutes per day ...' The topic of the first paragraph has now clearly been signalled as information about the process carried out for the assignment.

The topic sentence in paragraph two would then have become redundant because the information would have been moved to paragraph one. As it happened, the second sentence of paragraph two made a better topic sentence: "Child A talked a lot during her work", although we might have wanted a more general phrase about the child overall before getting down to detail: 'Child A was more extrovert than the other children in the group which was evident from the amount of talk that she did while working'. With either version it is now clear that the second paragraph is all about Child A (I prefer fictionalised names to letter or other codes because they are more natural for the reader).

You will have seen from Table 6.3 that the second paragraph originally contained at least two major topics, information about Child A and Child B. The paragraph also looked long on the page and in fact was about 200 words (which is two-fifths of the whole assignment), suggesting that it needed to be split. Halfway through the paragraph the topic changed: "However,

Table 6.4   The links between the research report structure and the example of an assignment

Paragraph and links with research report structure	Topic of paragraph	First (topic) sentence
1 Methods	First practice, observations	During my first placement I recorded observations of two children in the year one class where I was working. The observations were carried out for 10 minutes per day ...
2 Findings	Child A	Child A had an extrovert personality which was evident from the amount of talk that she did while working.
3 Findings	Child B	Child B was a quiet child ...
4 Findings	Target-setting	Targets were set with the class teacher for each of the two children.

Child B was very different she was ..." This was the perfect point to split the paragraph. A better start to paragraph three would have been: 'Child B was a quiet child ...'

Paragraph four began with the same weak phrase as the opening sentence ("For this assignment ..."); repetition is something that you should always be on your guard for because if used unintentionally it appears weak. The best way to improve the sentence is simply to delete the first three words of the topic sentence: and use the rest: 'Targets were set with the class teacher for each of the two children'. Having carried out these changes the structure is much improved. Jean's concluding paragraph was a good one which summarised the main things that she had learned by carrying out the work.

Despite the fact that the example was a different kind of assignment from the research report covered at the beginning of this chapter, Table 6.4 shows that there are clear links between the two forms.

DOS AND DON'TS

✓ **Do**

- think carefully about the overall structure of your writing

- use subheadings to title meaningful sections

- make sure that your paragraphs are complete, are the appropriate length and link together well

✗ **Don't**

- write one draft and think that the structure will be OK without revision and planning

- have paragraphs which are too long or too short

- repeat phrases and sentences by mistake

7 Grammar

The use of grammar is an essential part of the writing process. Having been shown the difference between prescriptive and descriptive grammar you will see examples of many pitfalls. Common mistakes made by students are shown and the use of the grammar check on a word processor is examined.

To start you thinking about grammar here are a couple of puzzles to solve. Can you think of a grammatical sentence for each of these:

a) a sentence with the word 'and' repeated five times in succession;

b) a sentence with the word 'had' repeated nine times in succession?

Answers at the end of the chapter.

Grammar is one of the most important parts of writing. It is the way that words and sentences are put together in order to express meaning. It is also one of those subjects, like apostrophes, neat handwriting, the Queen's English, and so on, that can make some people get quite worked-up! Here's a brief example.

My mother and father had come to visit one weekend and I was talking to them about the children. In the course of the conversation I said, 'The kids were sat watching the TV.' Here's a rough idea of how the conversation continued:

Mum: *Sitting.*
Dominic: *What?*
Mum: *It should be sitting. The kids were sitting watching the TV.*
Dominic: *No it shouldn't.*
Mum: *Yes it should.*
Dominic: *How do you know?*
Mum: *I just do.*
Dominic: *'Sat watching' has become standard English.*
Mum: *No. It's just wrong.*

What is it about parents winding you up?!

At the heart of all these kinds of arguments are different views about how language works. Some people believe that there is a fixed set of grammatical rules which you simply have to learn in order to speak and write correctly. People with this view can be called *prescriptive* grammarians ⊕. Most modern linguists take a different view. They see language as something to be described and analysed in order to understand the way that it is used. *Descriptive* grammarians ⊕ are interested in the way that all language use reflects a particular context, such as the social background of the speaker and the setting in which the message is communicated. This kind of information needs to be taken into account when analysing language and suggesting the rules that are at work. The idea that particular features of language are correct or incorrect is simply a product of someone's judgement, not an absolute rule.

⚷ KEY FACT

Claims about incorrect language use typically focus on a tiny proportion of the language. In other words, more than 99 per cent of our speech does not cause anyone to claim that it is incorrect but there are a few phrases which repeatedly cause disagreement.

The argument with my mother was based on a disagreement about one phrase. I suggested that although 'sitting watching' may have been the convention in the past, 'sat watching' was increasingly being used. The fact that language is constantly changing is a very important part of understanding grammar. If you accept this, it becomes illogical to argue that phrases are either right or wrong. But just in case you think I am suggesting that anything goes, the following sentence is definitely incorrect: rules are grammar no there for.

We need to make a clear distinction between talking and writing. Talk is much less subject to standard conventions than writing and tends to be more informal, although occasions such as formal speeches are a different case. Writing is subject to more agreement about what is correct than talking, although the internet and other electronic texts continue to challenge this idea. Conventional or 'correct' writing is standardised by various authoritative sources such as major dictionaries, style guides (including publisher's in-house guides and those available more generally) books like this, and computer packages/functions such as the grammar check. This greater standardisation of writing has occurred because there is the need for it to communicate without ambiguity to a wider range of people at ever greater distances.

★ TOP TIP

Think about grammar as a set of conventions to be learned rather than fixed rules.

Improving your grammar requires you to learn to proofread each word, phrase, sentence and paragraph in your writing separately. You also have to read the words and phrases in the wider context of the sentence and paragraph and think carefully if they fit properly. In order to write conventional grammar in your assignments you need to develop an 'ear' for academic language. In other words you will learn when sentences 'sound' right.

Improving your grammar can also be helped by recognising some of the common problems that students have and then applying this knowledge when looking carefully at your own writing.

Student example

A student was writing an essay about the national literacy strategy. Here's a quote from the essay. Cover the paragraph after next to see if you can work out the problems before you see the answers.

> *Various research evidence throughout the nineteen nineties looked at the teaching and learning of English and it was conclusive that pupils knowledge, skills and understanding in the area of English could be substantially increased. This was also evident in the results of the National Tests for English and therefore, the teaching of English education within schools needed improvement.*

> [1] Various research evidence *throughout the* [2] nineteen nineties *looked at the teaching and learning of English and* [3]it was conclusive *that* [4] *pupils knowledge, skills and understanding in the area of English could be substantially increased. This was also evident in the results of the* [5] National Tests *for English* [6] and therefore, *the teaching of English* [7] education within schools *needed improvement.*

So many things to think about in only two sentences! The first thing to say about the student's writing extract above is that the two points are good ones:

a) in the 1990s it was felt that standards of pupils' reading and writing could be improved;

b) the statutory tests (or SATs in everyday language) indicated that standards could be better.

However the good points are obscured by some of the grammatical problems. Let's have a look at each of the problems in turn:

1 Too wordy – the word 'various' is not needed. 'Research evidence throughout the 1990s' would have been fine. To keep the word 'various' and be grammatically appropriate the sentence would have to read 'Various pieces of research evidence' but then this sounds like there wasn't much research.

2 Unconventional – this is not incorrect but in a text like this it is conventional to put 1990s. Please note that there should not be an apostrophe after the zero (see Chapter 8).

3 Too wordy – 'and concluded that' or 'and it was concluded that' would be better.

4 Missing apostrophe – should be 'pupils' knowledge' because the student meant more than one pupil's knowledge.

5 Capital letters not needed – in general, capital letters are often over-used in assignments. The national curriculum is an interesting case. When it was first used in 1988 it was normal to use capitals (National Curriculum) but

since then the convention has changed to no capitals unless it is part of the title in the reference list.

6   Slightly ambiguous – this is not incorrect but the point would be stronger if 'and therefore' was replaced by the phrase 'adding further evidence that'. This has the effect of properly linking the second point about test results with the first point about research in the 1990s.

7   Too wordy – if 'education within schools' is deleted then the point is clearer: the teaching of English needed improvement.

Grammar check on the word processor

The grammar check does raise your awareness of some of the common problems, and for that reason you should try using it. But like all computer packages it has to work by using rigid rules. In fact the grammar check is a perfect example of how prescriptive grammar is an inadequate way to think about language. The biggest problem for the computer is that it cannot understand your intended meaning and the particular context of the points that you are making. This can result in some dubious suggestions.

Anyway, it's all very well me telling you what to do but let's see how good my own grammar is. I carried out the grammar check on the first draft of this chapter (which was changed considerably to reach the final version that you see now).

- The text in bold is the issue that the grammar check identified for me.

- The text in italics is the example from the draft of this chapter.

- The final text in the box is the grammar check suggestion to help me correct my work.

Extra spaces

Easy mistake to make and helpful to have it pointed out.

Capitalisation

Language is always changing and 'sat watching' has become standard English.
Suggestions: **S**tandard English.

Interesting; a perfect example of the way that language is constantly changing! *Chamber's Dictionary* says it should be standard English. The *Oxford English Dictionary* (OED) says that it should be Standard English but the examples of documents from 1836 to 1978 vary, with a trend towards using the capital letter in modern times.

Commonly confused words

Its just wrong.
Suggestions: It's

Whoops, bit of a typo there! The intended meaning was 'It is just wrong'. 'It's' is correct because it is a contraction of 'it is' (see Chapter 8).

'that' instead of 'which'

Unfortunately this mistake can be a keyboard error or 'typo', something which spellcheck ⑤ will not pick up because the spelling is correct.

> Suggestions: 'something, which spellcheck', or, 'something that spellcheck.'

The first suggestion ('something, which spellcheck') is nonsense and grammatically incorrect. The second suggestion makes no difference to the meaning. I won't be changing it but the publisher's proofreader might do!

Pronoun use

Which means that if someone tells you that you are wrong for using a split infinitive you can tell them not to be such a prescriptive grammarian.
Suggestions: him or her.

Publishers usually include guidance that tells us that we have to use words like 'them' in place of him/her to avoid gender-biased language, or in other words, sexist stereotypes so no change is needed.

Number agreement

If I spend that amount of time on two sentence I'll never hit the deadlines.
Suggestions: sentences.

Fair point, another typo there.

Compound words

when you are proof–reading
Suggestions: proofreading.

I don't mind that, it's easier without the hyphen. Language tends to be simplified over time so things tend to be missed out rather than added; a process called 'redundancy' (unfortunately the spellcheck offers both the version with the hyphen and the one without, which contradicts the grammar check!).

So overall it looks as though the grammar check has been about 50 per cent correct. Personally I don't find the grammar check very useful but you may find that it raises your awareness of some grammar issues. Make sure that you have the confidence to overrule it when it fails to understand your meaning properly.

If you look in the help menu of *Microsoft Word* you will find two useful documents. One is called 'Grammar and writing style options'. This lists all the errors that the computer grammar check looks for. It is too long to list in full in this chapter but in the section below called 'More common pitfalls' I will use some of the examples. The other useful document is called "Commonly confused words detected by the grammar checker". These are words like 'Advice/Advise'; 'Desert/Dessert'; 'Elicit/Illicit'. These are seen as grammar problems rather than spelling problems because they are actually spelled correctly. More about these kind of errors in the chapter on spelling but for now I just wanted to make you aware that the help document gives definitions for the different meanings of these words.

More common pitfalls

This chapter has already covered a number of common pitfalls:

1 Misunderstanding the difference between prescriptive and descriptive grammar.

2 Writing which is too wordy.

3 Not understanding changing conventions like '1990s'.

4 Not understanding punctuation (for more on this subject see Chapter 8).

5 Not understanding when to use capital letters.

6   Ambiguous meaning.

7   A lack of cohesion (the way that words, sentences and paragraphs link together to convey meaning).

8   Poor spacing and layout.

9   Commonly confused words.

10   Grammatical agreement for the number of things you refer to in the sentence. This is usually about singular and plural.

11   Compound words like 'proofreading/proof-reading'.

To conclude the chapter here are some others which many students fall into:

- Not understanding the subject that you are writing about – If you are struggling to understand some of the texts that you have to read to support your assignments this can result in poor grammar. If this is the case go back to the texts, read them again, list the key points and make sure you understand before you re-draft.

- Too informal – We all use the way that we speak to help us write. After all, writing is just a way of representing spoken language. But writing has developed sophisticated conventions of its own which mean that it is different from speech and generally more formal.

Here's an example of informal language: 'a trimmer condensed version was introduced'. There are two grammatical problems here. First, the word 'trimmer' is too informal. It is the sort of word you might use when talking to a friend but not when you are writing an essay. Second, the idea is repeated by the better phrase 'condensed version'. We call this kind of repetition 'tautology' which is basically saying the same thing twice. 'Trimmer' should have been deleted.

- Mixed tenses – As a general rule the tense should be the same throughout a piece of writing. Here's an example of a mixed tense resulting from a possible lack of understanding: '**In 2002** 80 per cent of 11-year-olds **are** expected'. The student was writing in 2003 so the tense should have been 'were expected'. It is important to remember that the year of publication is not just a convention of the author/date citation: it means the year that the text was written. As in the example above this can be significant to the point you are making.

- Which person? – Many people quite rightly point out that you should not use 'I' (first person) in an academic piece of writing (for example, 'I have found research showing that formal grammar teaching does not help writing'). Academic writing is often more effective when written in third person ('**Researchers** have shown that formal grammar teaching does not help writing'). There are exceptions to this though. For example you might be explaining what you personally did as part of teaching practice. It is perfectly OK to use 'I' occasionally but you do need to check how often and guard against over-use.

- Sentence length – If your sentences are too long you are more likely to be unclear. On the other hand too many short sentences can make the writing disjointed. Start the first draft of your writing with simple short sentences that are as clear as possible. Then work on making them flow. Sometimes you may join two short sentences together to improve the flow. Quite often the choice of the first word in a sentence can make the difference between disjointed sentences and smoothly flowing ones.

Do not be downhearted if you find that you are making some grammatical mistakes. All writers make mistakes. I once applied for a job as a principal lecturer, a job which I got in spite of the fact that my letter of application was headed 'Principle Lecturer'. That is the kind of principle that you believe in, not the principal which means 'head of'. Not bad for the author of a book like this!

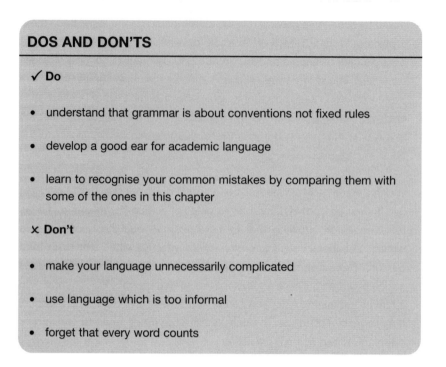

DOS AND DON'TS

✓ **Do**

- understand that grammar is about conventions not fixed rules

- develop a good ear for academic language

- learn to recognise your common mistakes by comparing them with some of the ones in this chapter

✗ **Don't**

- make your language unnecessarily complicated

- use language which is too informal

- forget that every word counts

Answers to puzzles

a) A fish and chip shop owner is replacing his shop sign but the sign writer writes 'fishandchips'. The owner says, 'you should leave a gap between "fish" and "and" and "and" and "chips"'.

b) During a discussion with two students about an assignment that they had just done the tutor raised the issue of whether a key point should have been i) 'Andrew had a lot of problems' or ii) 'Andrew had had a lot of problems'. Jill had used 'had' and Jack had changed his from 'had had' to 'had'.

The tutor observed that, 'Jack, where Jill had had "had", had had "had had"; "had had" was correct'.

Not the most elegant of grammar I admit! If you are struggling to understand the meaning of the sentence the logic is as follows:

1 Jack had originally used the phrase 'had had'

2 At the same point in the assignment Jill had used the phrase 'had'

3 'Had had' was the correct phrase.

8 Punctuation

Punctuation marks are small in size yet very important in helping you to make your meaning clear. In this chapter you will learn about the purpose of all the main punctuation marks. In order to help you think about your own use of punctuation you will also read about the kinds of errors that students often make with punctuation marks.

The most basic punctuation mark is the full stop. We often say that a full stop is used to mark the end of a sentence but this begs the question 'what is a sentence?' ☻ People often say that a sentence is something that begins with a capital letter and ends with a full stop. This is a bit of a circular description if we are trying to explain a full stop: a full stop is used at the end of a sentence and a sentence has a full stop at the end! It is also linguistically inaccurate. Sentences sometimes end with question marks or exclamation marks. Many printed sentences lack punctuation, such as newspaper headlines. Spoken sentences do not have a capital letter and a full stop either. Having said that it is very rare that we speak in the exact equivalent of written sentences; speech has different organisational and structural features.

Defining a sentence is not easy but the work of David Crystal (2004) is very helpful for this discussion. A sentence is:

- A construction which can be used on its own, without people feeling that it is incomplete.

- The largest construction to which the rules of grammar apply (in a descriptive sense, see Chapter 7).

- Constructed according to a system of rules which are naturally acquired by nearly all the mother-tongue speakers of the language. A sentence formed in this way is said to be grammatical. (Crystal, 2004: 37)

Minor sentences such as 'Hello'. 'Eh?' 'Like father, like son'. 'Wish you were here'. 'Taxi!' are irregular. Major sentences are what we usually mean when we refer to sentences. There are two types of major sentence: a simple sentence or a multiple sentence.

A simple sentence contains one clause. A clause must contain a verb and is built from 'clause elements' (which consist of one or more words).

Clause Element	Subject	Verb	Object
Clause (also a simple sentence in this example)	You	threw	a stone.

ℹ KEY FACT

Clauses can have the following elements:

- Subject (S)
- Verb (V)
- Object (O)
- Complement (C) (further information about another clause element)
- Adverbial (A) (further information about situation)

> ▶ There are seven basic clause types: S+V; S+V+O; S+V+C; S+V+A; S+V+O+O; S+V+O+C; S+V+O+A.

A multiple sentence contains more than one clause. There are two main types:

1 A *Compound* sentence: The clauses, which could in principle stand as sentences on their own, are linked by coordinators such as 'and', 'or', 'but'. For example, *'I like his hat* [main clause] but *I don't like his coat.'* [main clause].

2 A *Complex* sentence: The clauses are linked by subordination with words like 'because', 'when', 'although'. One clause (the subordinate clause) is subordinated to another (the main clause). The subordinate clause cannot stand as a sentence on its own because it relies grammatically on another clause. The information it contains is in the background compared to the main clause. For example, *'I answered the door* [main clause] *when Jane rang the bell'* [subordinate clause]. (Crystal, 2004: 201)

All of that was a slightly lengthy explanation of why a sentence is not just something that begins with a capital letter and ends with a full stop! The simplest and most accurate description of a sentence for children is that it is something which makes complete sense on its own and that *usually* it begins with a capital letter and ends with a full stop.

★ TOP TIP

You may feel that the terminology is a bit confusing. You do not need to remember the terminology to write well, if you develop a good ear for language. However it is useful professionally, when you are reading about linguistic issues or talking about them, because it can help you describe language more succinctly.

The first step in using punctuation better is to know what the main punctuation marks are used for. Most of the explanations for these are more straightforward than the one for the full stop.

Comma ,

Separates clauses and clause elements in a sentence in order to clarify meaning and to avoid ambiguity. If you read one of your sentences and it does not quite make sense look at the use of commas and either delete or add a comma. Commas have many other uses but are used particularly to separate items in a list or items in sentences which have list-like structures. The comma indicates a slight pause in the flow of the sentence when reading aloud.

Semicolon ;

Separates main clauses that are not joined by a *coordinator* which the semicolon replaces. The two parts of the sentence feel equally important. Represents a break in the flow of the sentence which is stronger than a comma but weaker than a full stop. For example, The students in the first study were hard working; those in the second were lazy.

KEY FACT

A *coordinator* Ⓖ is a word which links parts of a sentence. The most common coordinators are 'and', 'or' and 'but'. Some people call these conjunctions.

Colon :

Separates a first clause, which could stand as a sentence, from a final phrase or clause that extends or illustrates the first clause. Most commonly used to introduce things, like lists or an example. See paragraph one of this chapter for an example of the use of a colon and a semicolon mid-sentence. If in doubt do not use a colon mid sentence, reword or try a comma instead.

★ TOP TIP

If in doubt about using a colon or semicolon mid-sentence try rewording the sentence or using a comma instead.

Apostrophe '

This is the punctuation mark that probably catches more students out than any other. There are four main uses:

1   Contraction: didn't = did not;

2   Possession singular: the cat's tail, the child's book;

3   Possession plural: the cats' tails, the children's books (as 'children' is an irregular plural word the apostrophe comes before the 's');

4   Possession with name ending in 's': Donald Graves's book (although Donald Graves' book is not incorrect).

Common errors include:

a)   'This first happened in the 60's'. – logically, 60s is plural not a contraction. However in the past 60's was used as a way to signal plural but the convention has changed to 60s in recent times.

b)   'Was that it's name?' – confusion between 'its' (possessive) and 'it's' (contraction of 'it is'). This possessive form is irregular and does *not* have an apostrophe as in 'Was that its name?'

Parenthesis

Can be indicated with dashes (–) or commas but most effective with brackets (such as the ones surrounding this comment).

Parenthesis means structurally independent words or phrases which elaborate the meaning of sentences and which are often separated by brackets ( ). Square brackets [ ] are useful in academic writing to indicate that the words have been added by you and should not be confused with the quoted source.

> The Literacy and Numeracy Strategies have, according to all those who have evaluated them, been strikingly successful at improving the quality of teaching and raising standards in primary schools. But we need to *embed the lessons of the National Literacy and Numeracy Strategies more deeply* [emphasis added].

Hyphen -

a) Links words or phrases to clarify meaning; b) indicates that words are part of a single expression. For example:

(a)   We must re-form the group

(b)   The children were involved in role-play

Dash

The length of the line is given different names. One name is the *en-dash* (–) which is used to indicate a page range: p. 23–35. The *em-dash* (—) is longer and can be used to mark parenthesis (see above). It can also be used to indicate part of a sentence added as an afterthought but I would recommend that a comma is often better for this. In reality we usually use the hyphen key on the keyboard for most of these uses because it is easier than using the insert menu's *insert symbol*, *special characters* function. *Autocorrect* normally inserts the appropriate dash but you may need to check this.

Slash /

Often used to indicate words or phrases that are used interchangeably. For example, the statutory tests/SATs were carried out on the same day.

Ellipsis ...

Shown by three dots, an ellipsis indicates where something has been omitted. Often used to show that part of the text from a quote has been omitted. Also used in fiction writing to indicate an unfinished thought or to imply continuation of thinking.

Quotation marks "" or ''

Systems for using single or double quotation marks vary, but whichever system you use it's important to be consistent. The advice I offer here follows the style of the top education journals.

Double quotation marks are used to enclose a quote from a published source of less than 40 words (use single marks within the double quotation marks for material that was enclosed in double marks in the original source, i.e. to indicate a quote within a quote).

Long quotations of more than 40 words (see Chapter 3) are spaced and indented, and are not enclosed with quotation marks (use double quote marks to enclose material that was in quotation marks within the original). If punctuation is part of the quoted material then place it within the quotation marks.

Italics are used to indicate the title of a book, journal, magazine or film. They are also used for the introduction of a new, technical or key term or label the first time it is used but not subsequently. Single quotation marks enclose the title of a journal article or the chapter of a book if mentioned in the main text.

Single quotation marks are used to show that an expression is in everyday use but that it is not academically precise. They can also be used to indicate that you are referring to the word or letter in question rather than using it as a normal part of the sentence. Single marks are often used to enclose direct speech in works of fiction.

Student examples

Let's look at some of the ways that students typically misuse punctuation marks.

Full stop

The girl was relying mostly on the story and her knowledge of language to help her decode words. Which is good because it means that she is using sensible strategies and understands what she is reading but the phonic errors suggest this is an area which could be improved.

The problem is with the full stop in the section 'help her decode words. Which is …' Normally you would expect the sentence to continue without any punctuation at this point. The student realised that if this was the case the sentence would be very long so tried to break it up with punctuation. This was a good idea but it required changes to the grammar to match the change to the punctuation. My suggestion would be:

> The girl was using her knowledge of the story and her knowledge of language to help the decoding of words. These were effective strategies which particularly helped her understanding of the meaning of the story, but phonic miscues suggested that her phonological understanding was an area for improvement.

The use of tense always requires careful handling; notice how I changed the example to past tense. The interesting thing here is the way that I have had to make a number of changes to the meaning in order to correct what appears to be a routine problem with a full stop. My own knowledge of the subject of the writing is an important part of this. Quite often a lack of full understanding of the concepts and issues that the student is grappling with shows itself in weak grammar and punctuation. These changes show that as with all things in the writing process it is not simply a case of obeying a rule.

★ TOP TIP

If your punctuation seems to be wrong it may be because your understanding of the topic you are writing about is not strong enough. Go back to your planning and think again about the points that you are making. If necessary do some more reading and thinking, then redraft your writing.

Commas

Over the last forty years psychologists discovered children know a lot implicitly about how language works, and they use this knowledge to form expectations about meaning from speech, along with written language as long as it is in a meaningful context.

The first comma is unnecessary because the meaning is clear without it. The second comma is also unnecessary for the same reason and because it provides an unnecessary break in the flow of the sentence. However, if you take the commas out the sentence does not communicate its meaning clearly, mainly because it is too long. The following is better:

Over the last forty years psychologists have discovered much more about children's implicit knowledge. Children's language knowledge results in them having an expectation that speech and writing communicate meaning. In order to derive meaning from written language young children in particular benefit from writing being part of a meaningful context.

Once again the problem is not simply one of re-punctuating. In particular, the point made in the final sentence is not sufficiently developed. It would probably need a new paragraph with some examples and further explanation offered.

Quotation marks

The "look and say" approach teaches children to recognise whole words rather than looking at the individual letters.

The quotation marks should be single because this is an expression not a quotation.

Colon (and a few other things)

Try and work out the mistakes in the following paragraph before you look at the answers. Once you have understood the points repeat the exercise, without looking at the answers, in order to help your memory of things to look for.

Smith (Smith, 1994) gave a few simple rules to the volunteers, 'If the mistake doesn't make sense, then prompt with a clue about the meaning of the story. If the mistake makes sense, prompt with a clue about the way the word looks. If the reader does not say anything ask them to read to the end of the sentence or go back to the beginning of the sentence again.'

Smith[1] ([2]Smith,[3] 1994) gave a few simple rules to the volunteers,[4] '[5]If the mistake doesn't make sense,[6] then prompt with a clue about the meaning of the story. If the mistake makes sense, prompt with a clue about the way the word looks. If the reader does not say anything ask them to read to the end of the sentence or go back to the beginning of the sentence again.'[7]

Here are the explanations for the mistakes:

1   Don't repeat the name for a citation.

2   In this context the bracket should be before the year, not before the name.

3   Comma not necessary if bracket moved and repeat of name deleted.

4   This should be a colon not a comma because the student is introducing a quote which extends the first part of the sentence.

5   The quotation should be moved to a new line and indented because it is more than 39 words long which means that quotation marks are not needed. They would be doubles if the quote was less than 40 words.

6   Comma not necessary but should be kept if the original source included it.

7   Page number of quotation needed. Quotation mark not needed if quote is set out appropriately.

Here's how the paragraph should have been punctuated:

Smith (1994) gave a few simple rules to the volunteers:

If the mistake doesn't make sense then prompt with a clue about the meaning of the story. If the mistake makes sense prompt with a clue about the way the word looks. If the reader does not say anything ask them to read to the end of the sentence or go back to the beginning of the sentence again. (Smith, 1994, p. 23)

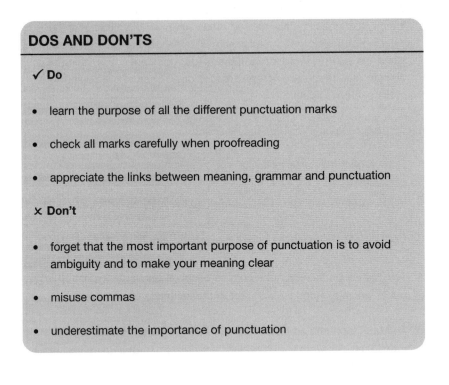

DOS AND DON'TS

✓ **Do**

- learn the purpose of all the different punctuation marks

- check all marks carefully when proofreading

- appreciate the links between meaning, grammar and punctuation

✗ **Don't**

- forget that the most important purpose of punctuation is to avoid ambiguity and to make your meaning clear

- misuse commas

- underestimate the importance of punctuation

9 Spelling

The history of the development of English has resulted in its spelling being difficult to learn. One of the first things that you need to think about is your problem words. You are shown how to think actively about these in order to remember them. You are also given other ideas about how to remember words.

Why is English spelling so tricky? It is mainly because it is not a 100 per cent phonetic language like Spanish or Finnish; a significant minority of its words are phonetically irregular. George Bernard Shaw cleverly illustrated this. Do you know what 'ghoti' means? The answer is 'fish'. If you take the sound of 'gh' in enough, the 'o' in women, and the 'ti' in station you get fish! It is the irregularities of English spelling that make it demanding to learn.

One of the main reasons that English spelling is phonetically irregular is because of the many ways through history that it has been influenced. It was during the fifth century that the Anglo-Saxons settled in England and as always happens when people settle they bring changes to the language, which was at that time 'Old English'. The texts that have survived from the period are in four main dialects: West Saxon, Kentish, Mercian, and Northumbrian. West Saxon became the standard dialect at the time but is not the direct ancestor of modern standard English which is mainly derived from an Anglian dialect (Barber, 1993). If we take the modern word 'cold' as an example, the Anglian 'cald' is the stronger influence as opposed to the West Saxon version, 'ceald'.

In the ninth century the Vikings bought further changes to the language. Place names were affected: 'Grimsby' meant Grim's village and 'Micklethwaite' meant large clearing. The pronunciation of English speech was affected at this time and it is possible to recognise some Scandinavian influenced words because of their phonological form. It is suggested that 'awe' is a Scandinavian word and that this came from changes of pronunciation to the Old English word 'ege'. One of the most interesting things about Scandinavian *loanwords* ❾ is that they are so commonly used: sister, leg, neck, bag, cake, dirt, fellow, fog, knife, skill, skin, sky, window, flat, loose, call, drag, and even 'they' and 'them' (Barber, 1993).

In more recent times, words from a range of countries have been borrowed. Here is a small selection of examples:

French – elite, liaison, menu, plateau;

Spanish and Portuguese – alligator, chocolate, cannibal, embargo, potato;

Italian – concerto, balcony, casino, cartoon;

Indian – bangle, cot, juggernaut, loot, pyjamas, shampoo;

African languages – banjo, zombie, rumba, tote.

However for many of these words it is difficult to attribute them to one original country. To illustrate the complexities of detecting where words originated consider the word 'chess':

> 'Chess' was borrowed from Middle French in the fourteenth century. The French word was, in turn, borrowed from Arabic, which had earlier borrowed it from Persian 'shah' ('king'). Thus the etymology of the word reaches from Persian, through Arabic and Middle French, but its ultimate source (as far back as we can trace its history) is Persian. Similarly, the etymon of 'chess', that is,

the word from which it has been derived, is immediately 'esches' and ultimately 'shah'. Loanwords have, as it were, a life of their own that cuts across the boundaries between languages. (Pyles and Algeo, 1993: 286)

The influence of loanwords is one of the factors that has resulted in some of the irregularities of English spelling. David Crystal (1997) lists some of the other major factors. Above, we referred to the Anglo-Saxon period; at this time there were only 24 graphemes (letter symbols) to represent 40 phonemes (sounds). Later 'i' and 'j', 'u' and 'v' were changed from being interchangeable to having distinct functions and 'w' was added but many sounds still had to be signalled by combinations of letters.

After the Norman conquest, French scribes – who had responsibility for publishing texts – re-spelled a great deal of the language. They introduced new conventions such as 'qu' for 'cw' (queen), 'gh' for 'h' (night), and 'c' before 'e' or 'i' in words such as 'circle' and 'cell'. Once printing became better established in the West this added further complications. William Caxton (1422–1491) is often credited with the 'invention' of the printing press but this is not accurate. During the seventh century the Chinese printed the earliest known book *The Diamond Sutra* using inked wooden relief blocks. By the beginning of the fifteenth century the process had developed in Korea to the extent that printers were manufacturing bronze type sets of 100,000 pieces. In the West, Johannes Gutenberg (1390s–1468) is credited with the development of moveable metal type in association with a hand-operated printing press.

Many of the early printers working in England were foreign (especially from Holland) and they used their own spelling conventions. Also, until the sixteenth century, line justification (lining up the beginnings and ends of lines) was achieved by changing words rather than by adding spaces. Once printing became established, the written language did not keep pace with the considerable changes in the way words were spoken, resulting in weaker links between sound and symbol.

The publication of Samuel Johnson's dictionary in 1755 was a very important moment in relation to English spelling. Noah Webster, the first person to write a major account of American English (and someone whose name is still celebrated in the most important American dictionary: *Webster's*), compared Johnson's contribution to Isaac Newton's in mathematics. Johnson's dictionary was significant for a number of reasons. Unlike dictionaries of the past that tended to concentrate on 'hard words' Johnson wanted a scholarly record of the whole language. It was based on words in use and introduced a literary dimension drawing heavily on writers such as Dryden, Milton, Addison, Bacon, Pope and Shakespeare (Crystal, 1997: 109). Shakespeare's remarkable influence on the English language is not confined to the artistic significance of his work, many of the words and phrases of his plays are still commonly used today:

> He coined some 2,000 words – an astonishing number – and gave us countless phrases. As a phrasemaker there has never been anyone to match him. Among his inventions: one fell swoop, in my mind's eye, more in sorrow than in anger, to be in a pickle, bag and baggage, vanish into thin air, budge an inch, play fast and loose, go down the primrose path, the milk of human kindness, remembrance of things past, the sound and fury, to thine own self be true, to be or not to be, cold comfort, to beggar all description, salad days, flesh and blood, foul play, tower of strength, to be cruel to be kind, and on and on and on and on. And on. He was so wildly prolific that he could put two in one sentence, as in Hamlet's observation: 'Though I am native here and to the manner born, it is custom more honoured in the breach than the observance.' He could even mix metaphors and get away with it, as when he wrote: 'Or to take arms against a sea of troubles.' (Bryson, 1990: 57)

Johnson's work resulted in dictionaries becoming used as the basis for 'correct' usage for the first time. Dictionaries have a major role in the standardisation of language and it is interesting to note that standard American English is represented by *Webster*'s dictionary but standard (English) English is represented by the *Oxford English Dictionary* (although *Chambers* dictionary is the main source for word games and crosswords).

David Crystal (2004) makes the point that although spelling is an area where there is more agreement about what is correct than other areas, there is still considerable variation. Sidney Greenbaum's (1986) research looked at all the words in a medium-sized desk dictionary beginning with A, that were spelled in more than one way; he found 296. When extrapolating this to the dictionary as a whole he estimated 5000 variants altogether, which is

5.6 per cent. If this were to be done with a dictionary as complete as the *Oxford English Dictionary* this would mean many thousands of words where the spelling has not been definitively agreed. Crystal gives some of the examples including: accessory/accessary; acclimatize/acclimatise; adrenalin/adrenaline; aga/agha; ageing/aging; all right/alright. Many of Greenbaum's words were pairs but there were some triplets, for example aerie/aery/eyrie and even quadruplets: anaesthetize/anaesthetise/anesthetize/anesthetise. Names translated from a foreign language compound the problems: Tschaikovsky/Tchaikovsky/Tschaikofsky/Tchaikofsky/Tshaikovski; particularly for music students.

The publishing process also has a significant influence on standardisation of the language. For example most publishers have in-house style guides for authors and editors. If you take citing and referencing as an example there are a number of different accepted ways of doing this with the *Publication Manual of the American Psychological Association* being a significant example of a style guide (see Chapter 3). There are also independently published guides such as *Fowler's Modern English Usage* (which isn't quite as modern as it suggests) and guides like this one which contribute to the attempts to standardise the language.

Examples of spelling problems

An influence on standardisation of language that has not been emphasised in linguistics texts is computer software packages such as the word processor. The computer spellcheck works by combining words from its dictionary with words that are in your personal dictionary. It has already had a positive impact on helping to reduce the number of spelling errors in students' writing. I am of course presupposing (and recommending) that you will use a word processor for your writing, although there are still some students who do their writing by hand which means that they cannot benefit from the computer spellcheck. Some professional writers also prefer to write by hand but they have the benefit that their work will be read by copy-editors and proofreaders whose job is to spot the errors and root them out. Unfortunately you do not have the luxury of a professional proofreader to help you with your writing, it would be nice though wouldn't it? The idea that writers work with other people to get feedback on their work is an important one. Although good writing is always driven by the main author, writers nearly always rely on other people as part of the complete process. So it is a good idea to work with your peers to support your writing (while ensuring that it is your own work) and in particular proofreading, including spelling.

The majority of spelling problems in education students' writing are more to do with grammar than a lack of understanding about how to spell particular words. Let's have a look at some examples.

> **Incorrect**: "will give the teacher ideas about were a child is in their learning"
> **Correct**: will give the teacher ideas about where a child is in their learning

Sometimes this mistake is a typo and in some parts of the country it relates to the way that 'were' is pronounced. Apart from the spelling/grammar problem the language of the extract is not precise enough. A better wording might have been 'will give the teacher ideas to assess the child's learning'; this avoids the original problem altogether.

> **Incorrect**: "investigating what areas where like in the past"
> **Correct**: investigating what areas were like in the past

The same error reversed.

Just in case you think that this is a rather basic mistake, here is a quote from the first page of the May 2005 edition of the British Educational Research Association (BERA) journal *Research Intelligence*:

> One of the challenges of the BERA conference is that different groups want very different things from it. Traditionally it has been seen primarily as a conference for the educational research community itself; a place were researchers, whether just starting out or well established, can talk to colleagues in a supportive and open atmosphere.

Incorrect: "which meant she rusted the activities"
Correct: which meant she rushed the activities

Definite typing error here. The 'T' is close to the 'H' on the keyboard. Unfortunately 'rusted' is spelled correctly, so is not picked up by spellcheck, but obviously does not make sense in the context.

Incorrect: "comparing the seaside now to what it use to be like in the past"
Correct: comparing the seaside now to what it used to be like in the past

Sometimes in the course of changing the tense of a piece of writing you can miss some of the other words that need changing.

Incorrect: "which is an on going type of assessment"
Correct: which is an on-going type of assessment

This is really a hyphen problem but once again the spellcheck does not pick this up, although the grammar check might do.

The problems with homophones

People who learn to write beyond GCSE level are able to accurately spell most of the words that they need to use. But we all have a number of words that we persistently misspell. Here are some of the words that I personally have wrestled with.

Effect and Affect

The way I sorted these out was through grammatical understanding. I mainly use 'effect' as a noun; to remind myself I think about 'special effects'. I mainly use 'affect' as a verb which might be used in 'the activity affected the pupil's motivation'. However, when you look them up in the dictionary you see that they can be used in a wide range of ways and confusingly both can be either a noun or a verb.

Practice and Practise

These two are important for education students who have to think about teaching practice and practising their teaching skills. As you saw in the last sentence I mainly use 'practice' as a noun whereas I use 'practise' mostly as a verb.

Principle and Principal

We need to go back to first principles on this one! 'Principal' can be remembered by the idea that an American headteacher is called a principal. Whereas 'principle' is something that forms the basis for thought and/or action.

Inquiry and Enquiry

A public inquiry is something that frequently is reported in the media. At the time of writing, the Rose inquiry into the teaching of reading had been announced. The *Oxford English Dictionary* says that 'enquire' is an alternative form of 'inquire'. Other dictionaries say that 'inquire' is standard English but 'enquire' is still very frequently used especially in the sense 'to ask a question'.

As I explained in Chapter 7 the grammar check detects commonly confused words and there is a full list of these available through Help (on Windows but not the Apple operating system at the time of writing) and it is useful to think about the ones that you struggle with. Here are two quoted from the list including the explanations given by the Word Help information.

Table 9.1   Thinking actively about problem words

Word	Difficult part	Breakdown	Similar words 1	2	3	4
There	er	t + here	here	the	where	then
Heard	ea	h + ear + d	heart	hear	earn	earned
Tomorrow	m rr	to + morrow	tomato	tomography	borrow	follow

Let's and Lets

Use 'let's', a contraction, when you mean 'let us'. Use 'lets', a verb, when you mean 'allows' or 'rents'.

Who's and Whose

Use 'who's', a contraction, when you mean 'who is'. Use 'whose', a pronoun, to indicate possession – for example, 'whose books are these?'

How to improve your spelling

Each time we use the computer spellcheck (or proofread our writing) we are given a reminder about the words we spell wrong. In order to learn how to remember these words we need to think more actively. Table 9.1 shows a framework for thinking about your problem words.

First of all you need to identify which letter(s) in the word you find difficult to remember. Next, try and think of a logical way of breaking the word into smaller parts. It can be helpful to think about stems, *prefixes* ● and *suffixes* ●. Finally try and use analogies with other similar words to help you remember the word next time. The key aspect of the similar words is that they share visual characteristics more than aural characteristics. In other words they look similar rather than sound similar.

> ### ☌ KEY FACT
>
> A prefix consists of a letter or letters placed at the front of a word or stem to form a new word: for example, 'before' 'be-fore'; 'be' is the prefix and 'fore' is the stem. A suffix consists of a letter or letters placed at the end of a word or stem to form a new word: for example, 'shorten' 'short-en'; 'short' is the stem and 'en' is the suffix.

You also need to develop a range of other strategies to help you remember problem words. Here are some suggestions:

1   Spelling 'Rules'

Although there are always exceptions to spelling rules the process of thinking about them and investigating the extent to which they work can help to improve spelling. One of the most well known rules is: I before E except after C when the sound is /ee/: for example, 'field' or 'receive'.

Another rule is that for words ending with a single consonant, preceded by a short vowel sound, you should double the consonant before adding the suffix: for example, split – splitting; bet – betted.

2   Developing the visual memory

Margaret Peters argued that spelling was largely a visual memory skill so she encouraged teachers to use the strategy of 'look, cover, write, check'. This involves looking at the correct spelling of a problem word, covering it, attempting to write it then checking to see if you wrote it correctly.

3   Mnemonics and other devices

Think of 'necessary' as two ships on the sea, or two sleeves and one collar (two Ss and one C).

4   Sound-out words as they look

An example of this is: /bus/ /ee/ /ness/ for business.

5   Use a dictionary

A good dictionary such as *Chambers* or *Longmans* is a fascinating resource. Look up your problem words and read about their different meanings, and the different grammatical functions that they have. Greater knowledge about words and seeing them in the context of the dictionary can help jog your memory when you next come to write them.

6   Play word games

Games like *Scrabble*, *Boggle*, *Double Quick*, *Lexicon*, crosswords, word searches and so on all require standard spelling. One of the interesting aspects of Scrabble is the way that very good players know all the more than 100 two letter words that there are. As part of your knowledge of word structures it can be interesting to look at the way that two and three letter words are built on to construct other words.

DOS AND DON'TS

✓ Do

- try the range of ways to improve your spelling suggested in this chapter

- use spellcheck

- think about how you can remember spellings

✗ Don't

- underestimate the importance of spelling

- ignore the words that you have difficulty with

- forget that English spelling has many visual letter patterns which can help you learn words

10 Presentation and Proofreading

You can greatly improve your writing by learning to proofread better. Having read this chapter you will understand the importance of keyboard skills and handwriting skills for exams. You will also learn some key messages about Powerpoint. The chapter concludes with a proofreading test based on a student's work.

One of the traps that many students fall into is to think that the more special effects there are in a text the more exciting it is. Shakespeare's comment that 'all that glisters is not gold' is relevant here. The best kind of academic presentation is one that least obscures the points that you are putting forward. To put this another way the presentation should simply enhance what you are saying by not being obtrusive. You should not feel that a piece of writing that follows all the conventions accurately is a boring one. On the contrary, if your message is well-researched and the language you use is effective this can be very exciting for the reader, particularly if they learn something themselves.

The internet has good examples of the principle of the presentation not interfering with access to the message. The best internet sites are those which are logically laid out and allow you to access their information quickly. They tend not to have dramatic presentation effects. Good examples of this style include the Amazon internet bookstore or the Kelkoo price comparison site. Berger and Wyse's site is much more artistic than these other examples but still has a simple logical structure combined with imaginative artwork, sound and visual effects.

I have argued throughout the book that I think that you should be using the computer for as much of your work as possible. This means that you will be using a keyboard rather than pen or pencil. Unfortunately, most people rely on two finger typing for something which occupies them for large amounts of their time. I would urge you to get hold of a typing-tutor package and teach yourself to type properly. When I started my teaching career I was increasingly using the computer to prepare school documents. I decided to try a typing-tutor package. At first it was quite slow-going and pretty boring but I persevered. By the time I finished the package I knew which fingers should be used for the different keys but I could not touch-type. From that point onwards I made myself use the appropriate keys when working on a document. Gradually, through familiarisation, I began to memorise the positions of the keys and the most appropriate fingers to use. I can now touch-type which means that my speed of work has been greatly increased.

★ TOP TIP

Teach yourself to type using a computer software package.

Handwriting

The time when you typically cannot use a computer is during written exams. This is when handwriting is a particularly important skill. If an examiner comes across a script that is very poorly written it does not put them in a good frame of mind. Primarily this is because they are under pressure to ensure that all scripts are marked to a deadline. A poorly written script means that they will have to take much longer to read it. Although this should not affect your mark if the points that you make are appropriate, poor presentation like this does have a subconscious negative impact on the marker. I even once heard an apocryphal story of an examiner who was under so much pressure that they decided to award an overall mark to each of the scripts based on handwriting alone! So, if your handwriting is poor you should do something about it.

The goal of improving your handwriting should be towards a legible, fluent and comfortable style. Learning to form the individual letters of the alphabet and produce legible handwriting at a reasonable speed involves complex perceptuo-motor skills. Sassoon (2003) puts forward the concepts behind our writing system. Direction, movement and height are all crucial: left to right and top to bottom; the fact that letters have prescribed flowing movements with specific starting and exit points; the necessity to ensure that letters have particular height differences. In addition, the variance between upper and lower case must be recognised and correct spacing consistently applied. She suggests that speed – but not too much speed – is also important as this can lead to fluency and greater efficiency. In exams it is necessary to think and write reasonably quickly.

Sassoon also advocates different levels of handwriting at different times. A calligraphic standard for special occasions might require a careful, deliberate approach which will be more time-consuming than a legible day-to-day hand. There are also times when you are drafting text or making notes, that you alone will read, where a lower standard of legibility will be appropriate.

In order to focus your attention on some of the key features of handwriting it is helpful to define some terms. *Ascenders* are the vertical lines that rise above the mid-line (or x-line) on letters like 'd'; *descenders* are the vertical lines that hang below the baseline on letters like 'g'. Most letters have an 'entry stroke' where you start the letter and an *exit stroke*. Some letters like 'i' may not have entry or exit strokes and are called *sanserif*, meaning without the stroke (the origin of serif is obscure but possibly came from a Dutch word). The letter 't' is interesting in that its horizontal line is called a *crossbar* and the height of the letter should only be three quarters. This means that the top of the letter finishes between the mid-line and the ascender line.

You will have worked out that there are four important horizontal lines: the *descender line*, the *baseline*, the *mid-line* and the *ascender line*. For adults only the baseline is visible; for children other lines have to be used carefully because there is a danger that they can measure the length of a stroke by the distance to the line and not by understanding the differences in letter size.

Sassoon (2003) recommends learning the handwriting joins in the following families of letters:

- Letters which join easily from the baseline: acdehiklmntu

- Letters which join easily from the top or the crossbar: orvw ft

- Letters which can be joined with loops if you wish: yjgf

- Other letters where joins are optional: bpqu

- Letters that are better not joined: zxs

- Joined with a movement which goes over the top and back except for E: ia ic id ig io iq ie

- Capital letters can also be grouped in families although they do not join:

  (i)   Straight lines: ILT FEH

  (ii) Line and arch: UJ

  (iii) Circular: CUQGD PRB

  (iv) Diagonal: NMVWYAKX

  (v)   Counterchange: SZ

Posture and working space are important elements of handwriting. For right-handed people the paper is tilted to about 45 per cent anticlockwise. It is important that the writing implement is not gripped too hard as this can lead to muscle tension in the shoulder and pain in the wrist and hand. Left-handed handwriting requires the paper to be turned clockwise to about 45 per cent and avoidance of holding the pen or pencil too near to the point.

Presentations

In addition to written assignments and exams many students are encouraged to give presentations, which may or may not be assessed. The main function of a presentation is oral communication about a topic. It is important to remember the word 'oral' in this context. The worst kind of presentations that I have seen are those which feature the presenter simply reading aloud a script. Students who come for interview are penalised if they do this in their presentations just as you would be penalised in an assessed presentation. However nerve-wracking it is, you must develop the confidence to move away from reading aloud from a script. The few examples where this is necessary include television presenters who have to do this because of the challenges of live television. The autocue reminds them of the words that they have to say. High level politicians frequently have to rely on scripts (often written by other people) because it is difficult for them to improvise on the many subjects that they have ultimate responsibility for.

Presentation software such as *Powerpoint* has become very popular. Powerpoint can be used effectively as an aide-memoire when you are giving a presentation. At its most basic you can think of Powerpoint as simply an electronic version of the overhead transparency (OHT) and overhead projector (OHP). One of the main benefits of Powerpoint is the ability to show pictures of things like children's drawing and writing which you would have to photocopy for the audience at considerable expense. Powerpoint also allows the audience to have a visual reminder of what you are saying. But there are many things that you should be careful about when using Powerpoint.

The basic principle that I outlined at the beginning of this chapter, that presentation should enhance (and not obscure) the points that you are making, is just as true for Powerpoint as it is for a written assignment. One of the important things about any text is its overall structure (see Chapter 6); Powerpoint is just another form of text. You need to understand the structure of a presentation as a whole. The *outline view* in Powerpoint allows you to build the presentation in a very similar way to the plan for an assignment. This gives you a much clearer view of the structure than trying to build the presentation slide-by-slide in 'slide' view. You should take care of the hierarchies of headings which reflect the logic of your message. If you ensure that you have a logical structure which supports the things that you are trying to communicate, your presentation will be better than one in which the audience are struggling to see how things relate.

The use of images which form an integral and necessary part of your presentation is good. The use of *Clip Art* just for the sake of improving the look is not good, because the audience may be thinking what is the relevance of these images to the message? If sounds and music are directly relevant to your presentation then use them but the use of sound effects between slides does not really add much to your message. It is nearly always better to avoid the pre-prepared styles and use your own designs instead, because this is more likely to enhance your message.

Edward Tufte (2003) provides some very useful cautions about Powerpoint. Compared to text on paper Powerpoint has very low resolution. So if you are presenting information with a lot of numbers, such as statistical information, it is a good idea to photocopy tables for the audience. The quality, relevance and integrity of the content of your presentations are what you will ultimately be judged on, not how pretty they look. Impressive looking slides do not mask weak content. Tufte even showed that the choice of a Powerpoint presentation rather than a longer narrative structure was a factor in the death of astronauts in the Columbia shuttle disaster.

The choice of headings, arrangement of information, and size of bullets on the key chart served to highlight what management already believed. The uncertainties and assumptions that signalled danger dropped out of the information chain when the Mission Evaluation Room manager condensed the Debris Assessment Team's formal presentation to an informal verbal brief at the Mission Management Team meeting … as information gets passed up an organization hierarchy, from people who do analysis to mid-level managers to high-level leadership, key explanations and supporting information is filtered out. In this context, it is easy to understand how a senior manager might read this PowerPoint slide and not realize that it addresses a life-threatening situation. (Tufte, 2003: 10)

In other words, unnecessarily complicated hierarchies which were part of the presentation, and the poor use of Powerpoint resulted in vital information being lost which led to a lack of necessary action in relation to the disaster.

Proofreading

Proofreading is a demanding skill for all writers but it is one that gets better with thought and practice. Although my proofreading continues to improve I am still not as efficient as a professional proofreader. If you are tackling new forms of writing, proofreading is even harder than it is for forms that you are more familiar with. First and foremost it requires you to have the attitude that mistakes really do matter. If your attitude is that you don't really care, you will need to change it, if you want to improve. You will also need to start taking an active interest in the way that language works and its conventions. The fact that you have bought this book is already a really good step along the road to becoming a better writer! Overall you need to develop your ear for language and learn to read like a writer.

Learn to see writing as a series of drafts. When you are doing the first drafts you need to concentrate on getting the words down. Don't worry about errors at this point, just keep writing. There is no point trying to correct errors at the level of the sentence if the overall structure of the text has not settled (go back to Chapter 4 and read the section on retrospective planning as a way of checking whether the overall structure is ready). Once you are happy with the overall structure it is time to get down to the nitty-gritty. Or is it? One of the difficulties for any writer is detaching themselves from the message of their writing. If you try and move straight from composing to proofreading you may find it difficult because you keep attending to the message rather than the surface features of the language. If time allows, you should leave the writing for a while; the longer the better so that you can return to it with fresh eyes. Imagine yourself wearing at least two different hats. The first hat is your 'author' hat. When you have got this hat on you should work on the message until the writing says what you want it to say. Your second hat is the 'proofreader' hat. When you have got this hat on you must look carefully at every word and sentence to correct the grammar, spelling, punctuation and presentation.

As the deadline approaches it is then time to really get down to the proofreading. Try starting with the sentences in the first paragraph. Read each sentence one at a time and ask yourself after each one, is that correct? Then ask yourself, does it fit with the sentence before? Having got to the end of a paragraph ask yourself, do all the sentences in that paragraph belong there and do they relate to each other properly? Once you are happy with the sentences and paragraphs run the spellcheck and actively think about ways to remember each misspelling (see Chapter 9). Having done the spellcheck read through again looking for words that are spelled correctly but are inappropriate grammatically. If you are not very good at proofreading then in the early stages you need to say to yourself, is that word correct? If the answer is yes, move to the next word; if no, replace the word and start proofreading again at the beginning of the sentence. The same process has to be carried out to check punctuation as well. The good news is that if you work very slowly and methodically at first, then as you become better at proofreading you will get much quicker. A useful stage, if possible, is to ask someone who is better at proofreading than you, to have a look at it and for you to learn from their ideas by checking them against the information in books like this.

Proofreading test

I am now going to set you a proofreading test. The following passage was written by a student. There are 11 errors, see if you can spot them all.

School-based Assignment for Maths

Assessment can take place over various periods of time, which can provide the teacher with different types of evidence. Short term assessment is an informal part of every day lessons. Used to check that children have understood the main teaching points of the session. Medium-term assessment is done every half term and relates to the programmes of study in the National Curriculum. Medium-term assessment is planned for and included in the end of term lessons. Long-term assessment is done at the end of the school year, to review and assess progress made by the children (National Numeracy Strategy, 1999). There are two main forms of assessment used in school Firstly formative assessment which is an on going and informal assessment.

School-b[1]ased Assignment for Maths

Assessment can take place over various periods of time[2], which can provide the teacher with different types of evidence. Short term[3] assessment is an informal part of every[4] day lessons.[5] Used to check that children have understood the main teaching points of the session. Medium-term assessment is done every half term and relates to the [6]programmes of study in the [7] National Curriculum. Medium-term assessment is planned for and included in the[8] end of term lessons. Long-term assessment is done at the end of the school year,[9] to review and assess progress made by the children (National Numeracy Strategy[10], 1999)[11]

[12]There are two main forms of assessment used in school Firstly[13] formative assessment which is an on[14] going and informal assessment.

1   'School-*Based*' should be a capital letter because it is in the title.

2   The comma in the first line is unnecessary. Although this is a structural point I don't think that this sentence is a good one for the start of the paragraph (or the start of an assignment). A better topic sentence for the paragraph might be 'Short-term, medium-term and long-term assessments provide the teacher with different types of evidence'. This is much more to the point and properly introduces the reader to what is to follow.

3   It should be 'Short-term' so it isn't confused with 'term assessment'.

4   It should be 'everyday'.

5   No full stop, capital letter, or other punctuation required here.

6 and 7　These are correct. National curriculum can be lower or upper case.

8　Probably better to delete 'the' but this is more a stylistic point than something which is a clear error.

9　Comma not necessary.

10　This citation should be to the Department for Education and Skills not to the title of the document.

11　Full stop missing.

12　Leaving a line at the end of the last paragraph is fine but first line indents with no space are more conventional in academic writing.

13　Capital letter at the beginning of 'Firstly' is incorrect. This might be a good point for a colon followed by the point about formative assessment then a point about summative assessment. This could be done using 'firstly' and 'secondly' although I find this a bit old-fashioned. Another option is to use list features like 'a)' and 'b)' but the sentence would work fine with: 'There are two main forms of assessment used in school: formative assessment which is an on-going informal type of assessment, and summative assessment which ...'

14　Should be 'on-going'.

And that was only one paragraph plus a bit more. Don't worry if you are slow at first, as I have said you will get quicker. If you really do not have time to proofread every word of an assignment to this level then make sure you look at the first page in particular. When examiners look at an assignment they often scrutinise the first page particularly carefully. If they find a lot of errors then they are more likely to look at the proofreading of the other pages.

DOS AND DON'TS

✓ **Do**

- remember that effective presentation is often simple and logical

- learn to type properly

- understand the limitations of Powerpoint in addition to the advantages

✗ **Don't**

- leave the proofreading too close to the assignment deadline

- let worries about errors interrupt the flow of your writing in the early drafts

- forget the importance of legible handwriting for exams

11 Assessment and Learning from Feedback

Before you start work on an assignment you must clearly understand what is expected and the criteria that will be used to mark the work. This chapter explains how assessment systems work by giving an example of a typical assignment. You are also shown two different kinds of feedback and given advice on how to learn from feedback.

One of the most common causes of poor marks is the failure to understand the requirements of an assignment. Before you start work make sure that you clearly understand what is expected by reading and re-reading the information provided in the course handbooks. Pay close attention in any session where you are given guidance on the assignment. If having done this and read the information carefully you are still unsure then make an appointment to see a tutor. A marker cannot give you any marks at all if you have not carried out what is required.

Assuming that you are clear about what is expected overall you need to turn your attention to the assessment criteria; it is these that the marker will use to arrive at a judgement. Although all assignments will have assessment criteria, the way that these are represented, the number of criteria, and how the marker arrives at a judgement vary on different courses. One general idea that is common to all courses is the notion of progression. For example, for a degree course there is an expectation that the assessment demands for each year of study are progressively harder. Year one is often called level one, year two level two and year three level three.

There have been, and there continue to be, discussions about the distinctions between these levels (and other levels as you progress to postgraduate study). Rather than get bogged down in the detail of this now, here are some broad differences. Level one degree work requires you to show a clear understanding of the main concepts related to the assessment topic and communicate this effectively through your writing. Level two work requires you to be able to critically analyse the topic in addition to showing clear understanding of the main concepts. Critical analysis means that you can weigh up *evidence* in a balanced way and then put forward a clear point of view. The word 'critical' in this context means not accepting things at face value. Critical analysis reflects your ability to challenge your own ideas by evaluating them in relation to experts' published work. This critical analysis could be based on your professional practice and/or reading of expert accounts of professional practice. At level three the particular requirement, which builds on levels one and two, is that you can synthesise theory and evidence. You have to show that you have read theory and research in significant publications and are able to understand, critically analyse and put forward an informed point of view. Frequently this also requires you to relate your reflections on theory and research to professional practice (for an example of how to synthesise see the student example in Chapter 4).

⚷ KEY FACT

Degree Work
Level one: Clear understanding of concepts
Level two: Critical analysis
Level three: Synthesis of theory and evidence

On some education courses the assessment is either a pass or a fail. On other courses a mark is awarded. Traditionally degree course marking has used the following scale:

0 to 39 marks is equivalent to resubmission or a fail

40 to 49 marks is equivalent to a 3rd class (III) degree

50 to 59 marks is equivalent to a lower second class (II ii) degree (the most common)

60 to 69 marks is equivalent to an upper second class (II i) degree

70 to 100 marks is equivalent to a first class (I) degree

There are general criteria for levels one, two and three which represent performance at these different classifications but it is very hard to link these general criteria with work that you are doing for a particular assignment. This is why I recommend that you pay particularly careful attention to the advice given and the criteria established by your tutors for specific assignments.

Traditionally, markers for degree courses rarely give marks above 80. It is not entirely clear why this is, although to a certain extent it reflects the fact that all assignments could be improved in one way or another. It perhaps also reflects the fact that you cannot put all your effort into one assignment because you tend to be working on more than one task at any one time. This means that there is a compromise in the amount of time you can spend perfecting just one of the assignments.

The way that marks are awarded varies. Some courses clearly link performance with specific marks related to criteria. For example if we had 10 assessment criteria for an assignment, it would be convenient to award a maximum of ten marks per criterion. If it was decided to do that, you could have a scale like this:

Outstanding – 9 or 10 marks

Excellent – 7 or 8 marks

Good – 5 or 6 marks

Weak – 3 or 4 marks

Very weak – 1 or 2 marks

A problem with detailed numeric marking systems like the one above is that some markers say these are too mechanistic and do not represent a realistic picture. For example, how could we justify that one student received six marks for a particular criterion whereas another student only received five marks? On the other hand these kind of systems clearly show the areas that are strong in an assignment and the areas that are weak. Some markers prefer broader indications such as strong, satisfactory and weak for each criterion which can be indicated with a tick, rather than a number, which gets round the problem of being unrealistically specific.

An important thing to understand is that no matter how rigorous the marking process and its *moderation* ❻ are, a *subjective* judgement is made by a marker/examiner. This means that it is possible that you may occasionally receive a few marks more than you should have and sometimes you may receive a few marks less than you should have. Students are unlikely to be disadvantaged by this overall because final grades reflect averages of marks awarded across many assignments marked by many markers. All institutions also have ways to deal with borderline final classifications which are often beneficial for students. The subjective nature of the marking process is the reason why students cannot appeal against an examiner's judgement. They can appeal against an assessment only if examiners have not followed the correct procedures laid down by the course and the institution. If students could appeal against examiner's judgements the whole system could become mired in endless arguments about marks and judgements. Markers already have to justify a proportion of their judgements through moderation with colleagues and external examiners.

ᵀ KEY FACT

Moderation is the process of checking that assessments made by markers are accurate and fair.

ᵀ KEY FACT

On average 10 per cent of assignments are moderated in order to assure the standards of marking. Dissertation marking often has 100 per cent moderation because it contributes so much to the final degree classification.

Assessment example

Let's look at an example of level one work. The assignment was as follows:

> Plan a sequence of three lessons in your specialist subject area for the age-group that you are going to teach on your next school experience. Write three lesson plans in the recommended format and a 1000 word rationale for your lessons. In the rationale you should explain why the activities are suitable for the age-group that you have chosen. You should also explain the extent to which you think the activities will motivate the children you are going to teach. You should discuss the ways in which your planning is related to the national curriculum and/or national strategy.
>
> The assessment criteria:

Specific Criteria
1 Appropriateness of the activities
2 Clarity of the links between learning objectives and the activities
3 Imaginative planning of activities and resources

4   Understanding of cross-curricular links
5   Likelihood that activities will motivate children
6   Understanding of links with national curriculum and/or national strategy
7   Evidence of reading to support rationale

General Level One Criteria
8   Clear understanding of concepts
9   Well-structured submission (for example, sequence of ideas; paragraphs; headings)
10   Effective presentation, proofreading, grammar and referencing

This kind of assignment is common on education courses because it links work done on the course with school experience. One of its positive features is that it encourages preparation for and thought about teaching prior to work done with children. The disadvantage of this kind of assignment is that it is difficult to plan activities for children until you are working with them. Day-to-day assessments and evaluations make it much easier to plan because you have more informed knowledge about what the children will require next.

In view of what I said above about understanding what is required, if you only submitted two lessons plans for this assignment you would lose marks. If you did not submit the rationale you would probably only be able to achieve a maximum of about 25 marks out of 100 which would not be enough to pass. If you failed to show that you had done any background reading you would score zero marks for criterion point seven and would be deducted marks for points six and ten.

Here are my suggestions for how you would meet the criteria. The choice of activities for the children is central to the assignment, hence criterion point one. My first step would be to search the internet for ideas including the government's sites that support the different subjects. There is a wealth of material here as well as many activity suggestions. The advantage of government sites is that clear links are made between the activities and the national curriculum so criterion point two can be more easily addressed.

★ TOP TIP

Try the standards site at http://www.standards.dfes.gov.uk for teaching ideas supported by government.

Point one should also have been met by using official activity suggestions but you would have to make sure your activities were suitable for the age-group that you had selected. Your activities would also need to show a logical sequence. Assessment criterion points three and five would be met if you showed that you had thought about ways that the activities would motivate children – this probably requires at least one paragraph per lesson in the rationale. Official activity suggestions can often be improved, in particular by thinking about what is more likely to motivate children in the context of the school you will be teaching in. This can show your ability to think critically. Your lesson plan would need to show that links with other subjects had been made (point four). Points six and seven could be covered together through some background reading about the subject including its place within the national curriculum and some of the key issues revealed in relevant publications.

A student who met the criteria very well on the task above received the following comments in their feedback sheet:

The activities and resources that that you have planned are imaginative and very likely to motivate the Year 2 children that you will be teaching. I particularly liked the puppet-show idea. Your comments about the benefits of drama were supported well by your background reading. You could have used other sources to help you critically analyse some of the views that you put forward. Overall this was an excellent assignment.

Now let's look at a student who performed less well:

You chose three activities that Year 4 children are likely to enjoy. Your comment about the range of approaches to mathematical addition was supported by a useful citation.

Overall, there was a lack of evidence in the assignment that you had clearly understood the way that your activities fitted with the national numeracy strategy. This may have been the reason that they lacked an appropriate sense of progression. You need to do more reading in order to ensure that you have a proper understanding of the topic. Please look again at the referencing guidelines and ensure that you follow these. There were a large number of proofreading errors.

One of the best ways to improve your writing and marks for assignments is to learn from feedback. The first thing to do is to carefully read the comments. This might sound obvious but some students do not do this because they just consider the overall mark. When you first read some critical comments it is quite natural to go through these feelings:

a) irritation – how dare they treat my work in this way!

b) denial – surely there must be some mistake?

c) resigned acceptance – I suppose I'd better read the comments.

d) new learning – I have thought about each of the comments and some will help me improve in future.

You need to read each comment and look back at the assignment to decide whether you could have improved it. Then, most importantly, you need to think about how what you have learned from the feedback could help your next assignment. If you really do not understand why the comments have been made you should make an appointment to see a tutor. Do not attend this meeting expecting to argue about the mark. It is far better if you take a notebook and jot down as many of the suggestions that the tutor gives you as you can, with a view to improving the resubmission if there is one and/or your next assignment.

Feedback happens to us all

Just in case you are thinking that it is only students who have to deal with feedback, here is an example which shows that tutors have to as well. When I submit a paper to a journal it goes out to anonymous referees who are experts in the field. The better journals send you copies of these referees' reports along with the editor's decision about the paper (frequently this process takes months). I once sent a paper called 'The national literacy strategy: a critical review of empirical evidence' to an American journal called *Reading Research Quarterly*. It was sent out to four referees but the decision overall was split between those who wanted to accept and those who wanted more work on the paper or who thought it should be rejected. The editors suggested some changes be made and that it then be sent to a second group of referees, although the most critical referee from the first round was also used for the second round. By the end of the second round of reports there was still opinion both for and against publication. The reports ranged from comments like this:

> The argument produced in this paper is an exemplary contribution in the manner of the educational researcher as public intellectual. A lot of high-sounding stuff has been written about "public intellectuals", but this paper instantiates a highly plausible and responsible act of public intellectualism. The author has demonstrated that policy interventions and implementations can be challenged on their own terms, by means of careful scholarship and critical engagement with empirical evidence. This is a heartening paper, and it should prove also to be an encouraging paper for people working at the chalk face in literacy education throughout the English-speaking world. We have all endured the kinds of "reforms" exemplified by the NLS and its FFT. There are many teachers trying to work to the limits of their capacity and integrity under conditions they experience as inappropriate and not in the best interests of many learners. These people look to educational researchers to provide forms of critique and leadership that hold out hope for more expansive and balanced policy directions.
>
> This paper gives such teachers something to look to. It provides a role model for other literacy researchers. And it is the kind of careful, measured, fair-minded and well-conceived research-based article we can never have too much of.

(Anonymous referee, 2002)

My grateful thanks to that reviewer! But now look at the following comment about the very same paper:

1 I am not convinced that the attack on Beard is tackled in a fundamentally new manner; the argument is sound, but it has been heard for over two years from Hilton in the UK.

2 Stripped of its sweeping claims regarding alternative strategies, the paper is leaner, but relatively brief, and contains little that would be new for a UK audience. The points about the teaching of grammar are sound, but Beard

himself quotes much of this evidence – it's just that he then goes on to spend 50 pages in his book telling how to deliver the teaching of grammar.

3   The author's final point is a call for an 'urgently needed' new review that critically examines research and practice, and how the two are linked. The government did indeed commission such a review in 2001, and it was published in June this year (see Harrison, 2002).

(Anonymous referee, 2002)

In the end the editors' decision was to reject the paper (for more information about the story of this paper see Wyse, 2004). However, this was not the end of the story. I submitted the paper to *The British Educational Research Journal* (BERJ). Once again the referees disagreed. One suggested urgent publication with only minor changes, the other suggested rejection. On this occasion the editors, having read the paper themselves, felt that the positive reviewer's view should prevail so they recommended publication on the proviso that the negative reviewer could offer an article in the same edition of the journal, challenging the views that I put forward. It turned out that the negative reviewer was the person who wrote the government publication that I was critical about in my paper.

I went through all the stages from irritation to new learning that I outlined above (several times), just as you may when you receive comments about your assignments. I learned least from the most critical reviewer for *Reading Research Quarterly* and rejected their comments but learned a great deal from those who were genuinely open-minded and rigorous. Although accepting critical feedback is difficult it can also be exhilarating once you clearly see that some of the points really are important and will help you to learn more.

To conclude this chapter, and the book, I want to leave you with a particularly happy ending! One of the students who I worked with carried out a piece of small-scale research which she wrote up as an assignment. She had been working with a child in a reception class who was described as 'selective mute'; this means a child who decides not to speak. This is challenging for teachers because so much learning happens through spoken interaction. Even the experienced teacher who the student was working with had struggled to support the child. The student took the opportunity to relate the practical situation to her final research assignment. She searched for research about the condition and was able to use this to develop strategies that she hoped would benefit the child. By the end of her teaching practice the child had started some limited talk with the student. This was a tremendous achievement. My comments about the assignment were enthusiastic partly because she had addressed the criteria very well but also because it was one of the best assignments I had ever read:

> This really was an outstanding piece of work. The integration of theory and practice was a delight. It was helped by the fact that this was a real problem that you wanted to solve but I think this assignment demonstrates that research, theory and practice in combination offer a powerful tool for addressing problems in the classroom. It has also taught me much and I would like to keep this as an example for future students. Well done!

I hope that your own hard work and talent coupled with some of the ideas learned from this book will help you to achieve similarly positive feedback!

DOS AND DON'TS

✓ Do

- make sure you clearly understand the assessment requirements

- learn from any sessions which are designed to support your planning for the assignment

- read feedback and learn from it

✗ Don't

- forget to check that you are addressing all the assessment criteria

- look at the mark for an assignment and not the feedback

- assume that you cannot improve in future if you have struggled with an assignment

Glossary

The definitions below refer to their use within the context of this book:

A paper Is an article published in an academic journal. Some papers are presented at academic conferences prior to publication.

A search A systematic way to find texts.

American Psychological Association (APA) 5th Style A set of conventions for writing academic papers, including referencing, that have been set out in a book by the American Psychological Association.

Anecdotal evidence Information that we gather in our daily lives that informs our beliefs about the world.

Author/Date system A way of referring to texts. The author's surname is followed by the year of publication.

Bibliography/Annotated Bibliography An alphabetic list at the end of a text which gives all the information that a reader needs if they want to read the texts that the author had referred to. Includes items that were read but not cited in the text. An annotated bibliography is a bibliography with descriptive notes about the text after the entry in the list.

British Educational Index A search tool dedicated to education that enables you to find educational papers more efficiently.

Citation A citation is part of a reference. It is included as part of a sentence in a text and is shown by an author's surname and the year of publication of their text. A citation may or may not include a direct quote.

Consent or assent form A form which is filled in by participants in research to show that they agree to take part and that they understand the consequences of taking part.

Coordinator A coordinator is a word which links parts of a sentence. The most common coordinators are 'and', 'or' and 'but'.

Critical analysis Analysis that involves weighing up evidence in a balanced way. Critical analysis reflects the ability to challenge ideas by evaluating them in relation to published work.

Dissertation An extended piece of formal writing which explores a topic in depth and is usually based upon original research. The term is related to the word 'discourse'.

Et al. Literally means 'and others'. Can be used to shorten a reference to a text with many authors.

The field An academic area of study.

Grammarian, descriptive People who see language as something to be described and analysed in order to understand the way that it is used. Descriptive grammarians are interested in the way that all language use reflects a particular context, such as the social background of the speaker and the setting in which the message is communicated.

Grammarian, prescriptive People who believe that there is a fixed set of grammatical rules which you have to learn in order to speak and write correctly.

Handbook A book which is typically international in scope so has contributors from around the world who are experts in the field. It attempts to be comprehensive in order to establish a clear picture of the field at a particular moment in time.

Hyperlink   A word or picture in an electronic document which is electronically linked to another document, or a place in the same document.

Inter-library loan   A library service which allows you to borrow books or receive photocopies of journal articles that are not available in your university or college library.

Jargon   Often used negatively to mean unusual words and phrases which confuse people. All areas of study use jargon to succinctly sum up ideas that will be understood by the expected audience.

Keyword   A word which is used during searches to access documents that are related to the keyword or which contain the keyword.

Loanwords   Words from other languages that have entered the English language.

Moderation   The process of agreeing whether assessment procedures are accurate.

Peer-review   A process designed to assess the quality of research papers. Papers are sent to experts in the field who read them then recommend publication or not.

Prefix   A prefix consists of a letter or letters placed at the front of a word or stem to form a new word: for example, 'before' 'be-fore'; 'be' is the prefix and 'fore' is the stem.

Primary source   The original text. One that has been read first hand.

Reference list   An alphabetic list at the end of a text which gives all the information that a reader needs if they want to read the texts that the author has referred to.

Retrospective plan   A retrospective plan is one that is written after you have done a draft of writing. It involves updating a plan after a draft.

Search engine A piece of software which enables you to find particular information by using keywords. Usually applied to internet searches.

Secondary source Referring to a text by using another author's reference to the text because you have not read the original first hand.

Sentence A language construction which can be used on its own, without people feeling that it is incomplete. The largest construction to which the rules of grammar apply. Constructed according to a system of rules which are naturally acquired by nearly all the mother-tongue speakers of the language (Crystal, 2004: 37).

Sic Literally means 'thus'. A word which looks unconventional or questionable but which is quoted exactly as it was in the original version of another text.

Speed-reading A technique which enables people to read much quicker than normal.

Spellcheck A software function in a word processor which checks spellings.

Subheadings Headings which consist of words and phrases used to divide text into sections.

Suffix A suffix consists of a letter or letters placed at the end of a word or stem to form a new word: for example, 'shorten' 'short-en'; 'short' is the stem and 'en' is the suffix.

Theory Ideas which explain and summarise things. In research, theory is developed or confirmed by observation and experiment.

Track changes A software function in a word processor which shows when changes have been made to a document.

References

Alderson, P. (1995). *Listening to children: Children, ethics and social research.* Ilford: Barnardos.

Barber, C. (1993). *The English language: A historical introduction.* Cambridge: Cambridge University Press.

Bryson, B. (1990). *Mother tongue: The English language.* London: Penguin Books.

Buzan, T. (2003). *The speed reading book.* London: BBC Books.

Carter, J. (1999). *Talking books: Children's authors talk about the craft, creativity and process of writing.* London: Routledge.

Crystal, D. (1997). *The Cambridge encyclopedia of language* (2nd edition). Cambridge: Cambridge University Press.

Crystal, D. (2004). *The stories of English.* London: Penguin/Allen Lane.

Department for Education and Employment (DfEE) and The Qualifications and Curriculum Authority (QCA) (1999). *The national curriculum. Handbook for primary teachers in England. Key stages 1 and 2.* Norwich: Her Majesty's Stationary Office (HMSO).

Greenaum, S. (1986). Spelling variants in British English. *Journal of English Linguistics, 19,* 258–268.

Harthill, R. (1989). *Writers revealed: Eight contemporary novelists talk about faith, religion and God.* New York: Peter Bedrick Books.

Higher Education Funding Council for England, Scottish Higher Education Funding Council, Higher Education Funding Council for Wales, and Department for Employment and Learning Northern Ireland (2005). Rae 2008 research assessment exercise: Guidance to panels. Retrieved July 2005, from http://www.rae.ac.uk/pubs/2005/01/rae0105.doc

Kirby, P. (1999). *Involving young researchers: How to enable young people to design and conduct research.* York: York Publishing Services.

Pyles, T., & Algeo, J. (1993). *The origins and development of the English language* (4th edition). London: Harcourt Brace Jovanovich.

Sassoon, R. (2003). *Handwriting: The way to teach it* (2nd edition). London: Paul Chapman Publishing.

Tufte, E. R. (2003). *The cognitive style of Powerpoint.* CT. Cheshire: Graphics Press LLC.

Tymms, P. (2004). Are standards rising in English primary schools? *British Educational Research Journal, 30 (4),* 477–494.

Wyse, D. (2003). The national literacy strategy: a critical review of empirical evidence. *British Educational Research Journal, 29 (6),* 903–916.

Wyse, D. (2004). And they all lived happily ever after? The story of a paper. *Research Intelligence (86),* 4–8.

Index

Added to a page number 'f' denotes a figure and 't' denotes a table.

LEARNING RESOURCES CENTRE